Risk Management Processes for Software Engineering Models

Risk Management Processes for Software Engineering Models

Marian Myerson

Artech House
Boston • London

Library of Congress Cataloging-in-Publication Data
Myerson, Marian.
  Risk management processes for software engineering models / Marian Myerson.
    p.   cm.
  Includes bibliographical references and index.
  ISBN 0-89006-635-3 (alk. paper)
  1. Software engineering.   2. Risk management.   I. Title.
QA76.758.M95   1996
005.1'068'1—dc20   96-35955
                                                          CIP

British Library Cataloguing in Publication Data
Myerson, Marian
  Risk management processes for software engineering models
  1. Software engineering   2. Risk management
  I. Title
  005.1'0681

  ISBN 0-89006-635-3

Cover and text design by Darrell Judd

© 1996 ARTECH HOUSE, INC.
685 Canton Street
Norwood, MA 02062

International Standard Book Number: 0-89006-635-3
Library of Congress Catalog Card Number: 96-35955

10 9 8 7 6 5 4 3 2 1

Contents

Chapter 10

Safeguards 161

Chapter 11

Economic analysis 179

Chapter 12

Reiterative processes 197

About the author 215

Index 217

Part I

Part I introduces the reader to this book. It presents an overview of industrial espionage and other major risks, such as malicious computer viruses and low position on the Capability Maturity Model.

Chapter 1

Introduction

1.1 Overview

Improving the quality of software development processes and performance has become a priority for almost any organization that relies on computers and networks. Low productivity usually results in late product delivery, poor product quality, poor performance, cost overruns, and customer dissatisfaction. Frequent occurrences of low productivity of successive projects will cause an organization to receive smaller profits and eventually lose business.

Low productivity is partially attributed to unrealistic expectations that the progression of a software engineering model—from concepts to production—will always be smooth. They are often based on the assumption the computers and networks will never encounter risks in running the models. This assumption is counter to the reality that risks to the models do exist, such as industrial espionage and malicious computer viruses. It is a question at what levels the risks are considered economically optimal or tolerable. Management objectives can partially answer this question.

To increase productivity, many organizations have used various software engineering models as the framework for building the processes of developing the product. As the processes, products, and projects become larger and more complex and more distributed, the risks to software engineering models become more complex and more compounded. In addition, the technologies are evolving faster than the development of newer software engineering models and the countermeasures needed to protect the assets from adverse threats.

To better handle the risk management processes, a new approach is proposed in this book. It is a first attempt to apply risk analysis and management processes to software engineering models. It differs from literature that discusses metrics in risk analysis and other quantitative methods as process quality measurement tools.

This book discusses how a risk analysis should be conducted. It emphasizes security and management objectives in determining risk levels, additional safeguards, and probable costs of model assets. Various algorithms, economic analyses, and various scenarios are presented—for both information security and software engineering models.

1.2 Audience

The book is designed as a reference for researchers, practitioners, educators, and system managers in software engineering. They will find the book useful in the discussion of applications of risk analysis and management processes to software engineering models. The book can be used as a reading supplement for graduate courses and research projects at the universities.

Computer security and risk assessment managers will find the book useful in broadening their expertise with regard to software engineering applications. It can be used as a guideline for further discussions on applying risk analysis and management processes to different stages of a software engineering model.

The audience is assumed to have knowledge of probabilities, matrix algebra, software engineering principles, software development life cycle, and CASE methodologies, as well as working knowledge of computer security.

1.3 The book

The book discusses applications of risk management processes to software engineering models. These processes are applicable in each stage of the life cycle of a model. They are reiterative when the changes in risk impacts or conditions are economically significant.

The book is not about software risk management. This phase of risk management focuses on software and related risks to software development processes. Software risk management does not cover other risk types, such as

- Developer errors;
- Natural disasters;
- Disgruntled employees.

For illustrative purposes, these risk examples are brief. They are just as important as the software risks and are discussed in the book. The risks of developer errors may be attributed to

- Poor training due to budgetary constraints;
- Inadequate skills;
- Inadequate software tools;
- Ergonomic problems;
- Environmental problems;
- Excessive office interruptions;
- Inadequate documentation on other concurrent projects.

The risks of a natural disaster are greater when a project is located in a building near a river subject to low and high tides. Obviously, it is riskier to do the work on the first floor than on upper floors during unusually high tides or flooding seasons. The risks are even worse when there are no backup plans at distant sites or when a disaster recovery plan does not exist.

The risks of a disgruntled employee are obvious. The employee may excel in developing a software product, almost free of errors. However, if the employee does not have good relationships with fellow colleagues or management and gets dismissed from his job, this person may become disgruntled. He may destroy files and programs and deny service to authorized users by flooding the systems with senseless messages. The employee may use password sniffers to gain unauthorized access to computers and networks.

1.3.1 Management objectives

Another risk factor that is overlooked by software risk management is poor management objectives. Importance of the objectives is emphasized throughout the book. If the language in management objectives is ambiguous, not clearly stated, narrowly focused, or not updated, a risk management program will not work or will be poorly implemented.

Management objectives specify what methods and strategies should be used to determine what assets can be valuated, what risks can be identified, what safeguards can be economically implemented, and what levels of savings are considered economically significant in each stage of software engineering model. The objectives should also establish criteria for changing or risk methods and strategies. Feedback on management objectives from software development staff is also important.

To expand, redefine, and implement management objectives, business management must actively ensure that organizational culture to be changed significantly must be favorable to software development personnel. Management must ensure that favorable cultural changes will result in the staff's positive attitudes toward quality optimization and optimization goals (see Figure 1.1).

Like the objectives, the goals must be clearly defined and stated for continuous quality improvement. After identifying and applying risk management processes to software engineering models, management should be supportive of the staff to perform studies of the impacts of the changes in objectives, goals, technologies, requirements, and regulations on the processes. The studies must include analyses to predict software and risk changes in order to stay on the competitive edge of the technology market that evolves faster than the requirements and regulations. The results of these studies will provide as feedback inputs into objectives and goals.

1.3.2   Book organization

Initially, the book gives an overview of industrial espionage and other major risks and proceeds to the discussions on promises and problems with the models on software engineering and software metrics. Then, the book looks at the theories of risk analysis and management processes from various sources. It ends with examples of suggested applications of risk management processes to software engineering models. It is hoped the book will encourage a more widespread application of risk management processes to software engineering models.

Accordingly, this book is divided into four parts:

- Part I: An overview;
- Part II: Promises and problems;
- Part III: Theories of risk analysis and management;
- Part IV: Applications for software engineering models.

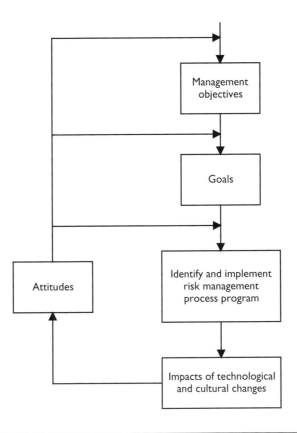

Figure 1.1 Management objectives approach.

The following gives more information on each part.

Part I includes this introduction and a chapter on an overview of industrial espionage. The chapter also gives brief discussions on malicious computer viruses and low position on the Capability Maturity Model (CMM).

Part II contains two chapters and covers the discussions on models and practices in software engineering and problems with software metrics. The chapter on software engineering takes the readers to two model types: software maturity and organizational maturity. The next chapter explains why software metrics is important as a measurement of software quality.

Part III sets the stage for the next part and presents two chapters on risk analysis and management methodologies. The first chapter covers methodologies used in the security arena. It takes the reader to the next chapter on various maturity models.

Part IV is more detailed and contains six chapters on suggested applications of risk management process to software engineering models. Each chapter focuses on each step of the risk management processes. They are, in respective order, asset valuations, security threats, security controls and tests, safeguards, economic value analysis, and reiterative processes.

1.3.3 Chapter summaries

The following provides the readers with summaries and important highlights for each chapter. They should help the readers with advanced background to select chapters of interest to them.

Part I: An overview

Chapter 1, "Introduction," gives the readers a glimpse of the book with a synopsis, summaries, and information on what knowledge the readers should have in reading the book. The scope of the audience is included.

Chapter 2, "Industrial Espionage and Other Major Risks," gives an overview of the subject matter. It starts with a discussion of how a company may lose the competition for a share of the market for its product if it is inadequately prepared for the consequences of these threats. The chapter follows with brief discussions on industrial espionage, malicious computer viruses, and low position on the CMM. The topics on industrial espionage cover various incidents of attacks on U.S. companies by domestic competitors and foreign powers. According to a 1995 report, various kinds of espionage have increased dramatically by 323% since 1992. They include strategic plans, research and development information, and manufacturing processes. The CIA and other intelligence agencies most likely have taken steps to increase their surveillance of the foreign spying activities of the U.S. industries.

Many system intrusions and unauthorized accesses occurred, for example, within large high-tech firms and government facilities. A CEO gave Winkler [1] an assignment to simulate an industrial espionage attack in three days in "a high-tech firm with annual sales in excess of $5 billion."

As discussed in the next section, a computer virus has been defined in different ways. Indications of a virus infection are partially listed. Then, the chapter takes the reader to the section on the low position on the CMM. The section starts with an explanation of what the CMM is. The model is divided into five maturity levels and starts with high risks in the first maturity level. As the organization advances to the next level, more and more risks are reduced to acceptable levels. The first-level organization may be a breeding ground for disgruntled employees and a source of ad hoc conditions, such as inadequate project management. Risks at the second level include introduction of immature technology, as well as inadequate project resources and an inadequate set of software development specifications.

Part II: Promises and problems

Chapter 3, "Software Engineering," gives an overview and describes two maturity types in developing a software product: software maturity and organizational maturity. Software maturity refers to how well a software product has been developed in a software development life cycle. The concept of organizational maturity emerged in early 1990s in the software development industry. It considers the impacts of how well an organization can develop a suite of software products and improve the quality of development processes.

Software maturity is based on software engineering principles that state that the models of software development are derived from other engineering activities. Feasibility studies and product design are some of the engineering activity examples.

Organizational maturity looks at the processes of developing the product in an organization. The Software Engineering Institute (SEI) at Carnegie Mellon University chose its CMM from several software engineering models for discussion on organizational maturity of software development processes. The model is divided into five maturity levels—from chaos level to optimized level. A discussion follows on how the maturity framework of the CMM is applied to the People Management Capability Maturity Model (PM-CMM) and the Personal Software Process (PSP). The CMM presents a framework for a process management software, LBMS Process Engineer software, to automate software development processes.

Chapter 4, "Software Metrics," contains five sections: metrics in risk management, metrics in various maturity models, metrics in the CMM, metrics in the Orange Book, and other metrics approaches. The first section briefly discusses various metrics approaches in managing software risks. Risk management helps the developers to better protect their projects from disasters and to reduce higher risks to more acceptable levels. Grouping of risk management into two primary steps, risk assessment and risk control, is summarized.

Another example of risk management is risk impacts. After additional safeguards and countermeasures are implemented to contain or remove the risks, their costs of implementing are assessed. The impacts of risks are redetermined when serious incidents occur and when changes to computer assets are major. Other change examples include tighter budgetary and schedule constraints, new threats and vulnerabilities, and higher confidentiality level of a computer system.

Then, the chapter takes the reader to a brief discussion of metrics in various maturity models. It includes a list (taken from a study) of eight models that use metrics to measure process and/or productivity of a software development life cycle. Three of these models, including the CMM, are concerned with risk assessment. Discussions on the use of metrics in the CMM are covered.

The next section discusses why the metrics as used in the Orange Book are an ineffective tool for quantifying and improving the security aspects of software development process. Then, it takes the reader to a brief discussion on other approaches. One example is Dr. H. Rubin's measurement dashboard as the fifth generation of software metrics. Another example is the object-oriented (OO) software metrics that may be useful in interaction and incremental developmental processes.

Part III: Theories of risk analysis and management

Chapter 5, "Security," briefly reviews risk analysis and risk management methodologies for both computer and network systems. The methodologies vary from one industry to another, from one organizational entity to another, from one management group to another, and from one system to another. The purpose of any methodology is to remove or reduce impacts of the risks of threats to the systems. Common denominators among the methodologies are assets, threats, risks, vulnerabilities, and safeguards. Each is defined from security perspectives. A risk analysis process starts with the identification and valuation of the assets for a system. The implementation of the safeguards does not end the process. The process continuously receives the inputs of changes in the management of risk impacts in an interactive fashion. This risk management process stage evaluates the proposals of implementing new or improved safeguards to remove, contain, or reduce new risks.

Discussions on risk analysis methodologies give examples of asset groups, asset valuations, risk impacts of the threats, and replacement costs for both computer and network systems. Item examples for each asset category are included. The items can be added or removed to suit a particular system. An item can be declared by management as an asset. After the assets are identified and valuated, the chapter provides the readers with examples of security threats to the assets, such as natural disaster, sabotage, and fire. The identified threats and associated vulnerability assessments vary from one stage of development cycle to another and from one system to another.

While full risk protection is not always possible, a methodology can be applied to remove, reduce, or contain the risks. The abbreviated risk method is used as an example. The method permits for each threat category narrative statements on existing safeguards and vulnerabilities to the risks of threats and looks at the savings justification sheet scenario as an example. The risk analysis process for a computer system is similar to the process for a network system. The scope of the asset groups, asset identification and valuation, threat identification, and vulnerability assessment for network systems is somewhat broader.

Chapter 6, "Process Maturity Models," presents risk analysis methods and risk management methodologies that the models use—both from software and organizational maturity standpoints. Software maturity looks at how well a software product can be developed in a life cycle—particularly the identification and analysis stages. Organizational maturity focuses on how well an organization can identify and analyze the risks for all projects.

The section on software maturity category of risk analysis methods discusses Boehm's risk management tree, risk analysis techniques, risk items, compound risks (versus independent entities), and two models. The use of risk analysis in the spiral model determines the ordering of software activities. Cases on serious deficiencies in risk management are summarized.

Discussions on the organizational maturity category of risk analysis methods cover the CMM and related models, the CMM versus the Software Process Improvement and Capability Determination (SPICE) model, the TRILLIUM model, and the SEI Risk Management Paradigm. The SEI built the CMM to improve delivery and the quality of the products. The SPICE model looks at a process measure rather than an organization measure. Discussions of issues on layering the CMM on top of SPICE are covered. The TRILLIUM model grew from the CMM and is used to assess capabilities of telecommunications suppliers. The SEI paradigm was developed when the SEI recognized that risks exist in the development process. The risks, if not properly managed and evaluated, could compromise the project's expected success. The SEI has shown it is possible to adapt risk management within the framework of the CMM. Then the section explains how CMM provides a framework for assessing and improving the way organizations develop software. It takes the reader to the discussion of automated risk analysis.

The following come under the software maturity category of risk management methodologies: Boehm's risk management tree, risk management techniques, and the coordination technology model. The organizational maturity category looks at metrics in the CMM and the SEI algorithm. In short, higher maturity levels imply a greater degree of process improvement. A discussion follows on the limits of human resources in applying the SEI CMM in smaller organization risk management issues. Next, the section focuses on CMM case studies to increase the maturity of the software development process and cognitive bias of the developer's thought processes in applying risk management methodologies.

Part IV: Applications for software engineering models

Chapter 7, "Asset Valuations," discusses asset categories and valuations. Assets are redefined to include the broader scope of the development life cycle. Identifying and valuating the asset groups for each stage of software development life cycle is the first step in applying risk management process to software engineering models. If the assets cannot be identified, the risk management process cannot be applied. This first step overcomes the deficiencies of software metrics and asset identification and valuations in software engineering models. The asset groups serve as inputs to later stages of applying risk management processes to the models. They are divided into basic and customized.

Basic asset categories are tangible and serve as a template or a guideline. For a computer system, they include hardware, software, physical, and communications. A network system may required a different set of basic asset groups. Each category is further divided into subgroups. The range of subgroups may change from one stage to another in a development life cycle.

An asset category template can be customized for a project. Customized asset categories cover tangible, intangible, and mixed asset items. Tangible asset items are easier to identify than intangible asset items. Intangible items can be grouped into organization, technical, and external factors. One example of an intangible asset item is the IS plan compliance. To quantify the costs of intangible assets, a table of criteria should be developed to cross-reference the relative values with the replacement costs of the assets.

Examples of asset valuations in the abbreviated risk method are given in the data sheets on hardware assets, software assets, personnel assets, and documentation assets. The valuations should include factors that can change the original costs of the assets. Threat impacts and replacement costs justifications are included in the data sheets. Costs can change from one stage to another in the life cycle.

Chapter 8, "Security Threats," focuses on threats to computers and networks. After the assets are identified and valuated, security threats to the assets must be identified. Identifying security threat categories is the second step in applying risk management processes to software engineering models. Significant threat categories provide inputs to security controls and tests.

Vulnerabilities in the system that are susceptible to a threat attack may exist for one stage and not in another stage for the same threat attack. Impacts of threats on each asset category range from not applicable to very high. The templates can be tailored to suit a particular project or a specific stage of the life development cycle.

The chapter gives examples of tangible and intangible threats. Sample threat data sheets for the abbreviated risk method are provided for the first stage of a development life cycle. Each data sheet begins with a short and clearly stated threat category. The location of the threat must be determined. In addition to the category, each data sheet contains information on subcategory, type, scope, average frequency, and historical damage.

Threats are arbitrarily divided into three groups: natural, intentional, and unintentional. Natural threats are easier to group than intentional and unintentional threats. Threat examples include the natural threat category on floods, the intentional threat category on unauthorized system access, and the intentional threat category on communication threats (particularly in a distributed computer system). Also included are the unintentional threat category on lack of disk management controls, the unintentional threat category on unintentional software developer errors, and the natural threat category on power failure due to industrial espionage attacks.

Chapter 9, "Security Controls and Tests," gives examples. After security threats are identified, security controls of the tests must be identified to establish a more secure computer or network system. They determine what vulnerabilities can be identified to pinpoint weaknesses of the system that are susceptible to an attack or a threat (tangible or intangible). Identifying security controls and tests is the third step in applying the risk management process to software engineering models. Vulnerabilities in a system are redefined to include vulnerabilities for any stage of a life development cycle.

If the tests show that vulnerabilities exist, the results of the tests should list what additional security controls are required to reduce the risk to more acceptable levels. Additional controls will incur economic savings from having recovered the damaged, destroyed, or lost asset. Depending on the risks to which a system is vulnerable, some security controls and tests are significant, others are insignificant or not applicable. The more complex the system becomes, the more likely the risks to the system will be complex and compounded. The less complex the system is, the more likely the risks will be divided into standard categories. If security controls change in response to evolving technologies, changing management objectives, and expanding security policies, tests should be conducted to determine what security controls, previously insignificant, are now significant, and what security controls, unique to the system, should be added. The changes in security controls should result in greater economic savings in protecting the assets from the threats.

Security controls that are applicable to most systems may be used as standard templates. Examples of templates include a standard list of vulnerabilities grouped under a security control for the abbreviated risk method. As with customized assets and security threats, the templates can be tailored to suit a particular situation. Examples of assets that are vulnerable to a threat are given. The chances of some threats occurring increase as a network extends across organizational sites, especially if the sites are a great distance from one another in the nation and worldwide.

The chapter also provides examples of security controls and tests for the abbreviated risk method. Using the same data sheets from Chapter 8, vulnerabilities are provided for each threat. The number of vulnerabilities for each threat is arbitrary. The list of vulnerabilities need not to be the same for each stage of development cycle.

Chapter 10, "Safeguards," gives an overview of protections against the threats. After security controls are identified and tested, existing safeguards must be identified. If safeguards do not exist or are inadequate, additional safeguards should be evaluated for their cost effectiveness and recommended for implementation. They are used to counter the weaknesses of the vulnerabilities in the systems. Countering a vulnerability reduces the weaknesses in a system or a project to a more economically acceptable level of risks.

To identify what safeguards are already in place and what additional safeguards are required, one should keep in mind that requirements for safeguards differ among network systems, minicomputers, and mainframes. The complexity of safeguards increases as the network sends and receives data on diverse platforms across organizational and geographical lines.

The abbreviated method lists significant safeguards for each threat data sheet. The list is short for illustrative purposes. The safeguards are recommended to counter the vulnerabilities in a threat data sheet.

Examples of data sheets on safeguards are given, including impact ratings. Impact categories arbitrarily cover modification, destruction, and denial of service for each asset. At least one impact category is applicable to the assets. In any impact category, not all assets require a rating.

Chapter 11, "Economic Analysis," gives examples of analysis algorithms in a stage of software development life cycle in three main areas. One area focuses on computing the mathematical values of implementing additional security controls and safeguards to reduce the risks to acceptable levels. The second area of economic analysis looks at the savings justification of implementing the controls and safeguards. The third area, the most important part, is the return on investment (ROI) in each stage of software development process for each threat category.

Discussions on software engineering risk management, impact ratings, risk prioritization rules, and probabilistic algorithms give a background for mathematical values. Software engineering risk management looks at the cost, the schedule, and the technical elements of the software process and product. Software process and product categories are identified. Organization and risk culture are examples of software process categories. Examples of impact ratings on two threats are provided. Risk prioritization rules determine which threat category has a higher priority over another threat category and when impact ratings are identical for all assets. One example of a prioritization rule looks at the analytical hierarchy process. A probability algorithm discusses annual loss expectancy. A sample matrix format is included.

Savings are justified when implementations of the safeguards result in reducing the risks to more acceptable levels. Risk levels are determined by management objectives. They can change over a period of time. Discussions on return on investments have been not adequately or inadequately covered for some software engineering models in previous chapters. Several ways of computing total return on investment are available.

Chapter 12, "Reiterative Processes," looks at continuous improvements to the risk management process. Identifying the reiterative processes is the last step in applying the risk management process to software engineering models. They help in improving the ROIs to stay competitive in the changing market.

Reiterative processes in existing software engineering models are either limited in scope or virtually nonexistent. Conditions for continuing reiterative processes are undefined or not well defined. To broaden the scope of reiterative processes, an approach is proposed to include the reiterative processes as the step in risk management processes for software engineering models. Reiterative processes are used to manage new risk factors and changing risk prioritization in a software development life cycle and to improve continuously the quality of whole risk management processes.

Conditions for continuing reiterative processes must be defined and specific. They can change over a period of time or with a new set of management objectives. When conditions are met, such as safeguards implementation, they result in improved quality of risk management processes and show better ROIs in economic value analyses.

If the impacts of changing conditions are complex, it can be tedious to perform, by hand reiterative processes on prior steps in risk management processes. To improve the process of managing risks in large, complex software development projects, the entire risk management process should be automated. Advantages and disadvantages of implementing the automation are briefly discussed.

Reiterative processes, automated or manual, result in a substantial rework of the software development processes. The issue of determining the limit on reiterative processes arises. The chapter ends with sample data sheets impacted by reiterative processes and a discussion of feedback mechanisms.

REFERENCE

[1]   Winkler, Ira, "Assignment: Espionage," *INFOSECURITY*, Vol. 7, No. 3, May/June 1996, pp. 26–28.

Chapter 2

Industrial espionage and other major risks

INDUSTRIAL ESPIONAGE is one of the most significant major risks to software development organizations. Malicious computer viruses are another source of major risks. Both can result in massive denial of service to thousands of developers and project managers across geographical boundaries (see Figure 2.1). Often, because of these risks, a major software product will be delivered late, will exceed the budget, and may not contain the features the users expect.

The company may lose competition for a share of the market for its product if it is not sufficiently prepared for the consequences of these threats. For example, a company found that foreign industrial spies wiretapped communications lines and stole their major innovative development secrets. The spies, with more advanced technologies, were able to develop the product with anticipated features that the users would expect in less time. As a result, the company lost its major share of the market and ran into cost overruns when it changed

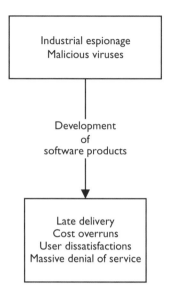

Figure 2.1 Major risks result in undesirable consequences.

features in their product and purchased technologies supposedly better than those of the industrial spies. Of course, the company went to court to sue for stolen trade secrets, marketing strategies, and proprietary development plans.

Industrial espionage and computer viruses are not the only major risks. Low position on the Capability Maturity Model (CMM) is the third major risk. This indicates that immature technology, inadequate resources, an inadequate set of specifications, and other project risk factors (see Section 2.3) exist.

Therefore, a risk management program is very important to determine how well the organization can respond to the threats to the system and having its resources impacted by the threats from industrial spies (e.g., the French government) and competing domestic organizations (e.g., the battle between Microsoft and Netscape over web browsers).

2.1 Industrial espionage

Evans and Morrison [1] suggest that "industrial espionage is growing at an alarming rate and is being monitored closely by government intelligence-gathering organizations." According to the FBI and CIA, the greatest threat to U.S. security is industrial and technological espionage by foreign powers—foes and friends.

Normally assigned to keep a watch on military subversive activities, the CIA has more and more monitored economic activities, particularly on computers, semiconductors devices, networks, and other technology areas. According to Betts [2], U.S. intelligence agencies, if given the authority, would monitor compliance with trade agreements. They would monitor for "subversive activities that might harm U.S. markets, technologies, investments, or research."

In Carley's article [3], the increased involvement of foreign intelligence agencies indicate that "the U.S. is a target because it is ahead in many technologies." Foreign intelligence services intercepted communications of U.S. companies, captured satellite signals, and tapped into government-owned telephones.

Greve [4] reports that "the French government, along with governments of numerous other nations, is spying on U.S. companies to obtain confidential economic information as well as trade secrets." The French government is not alone in spying to obtain trade secrets from the U.S. companies. China, Taiwan, Japan, South Korea, and Britain are other industrial spies. The French government engaged in the following spying activities:

- Placing U.S. business executives and defense officials in bugged hotels;
- Seating them on bugged Air France seats;
- Recruiting French employees of the U.S. Embassy in Paris;
- Placing moles in U.S. computer firms;
- Tapping phone lines;
- Looking through stolen garbage in search of industrial secrets;
- Posing as nondefense customers to obtain classified technology secrets.

As a matter of fact, Alexander [5] reports that "in 1988, the FBI uncovered an attempt by the French Exterior Security organization to hire employees at IBM, Texas Instruments, and other firms to provide information for pay."

The CIA and the National Security Agency most likely will increase its monitoring activities for the years to come. Many system intrusions and unauthorized accesses occurred within corporate organizations and government entities. This is a result of, in part, inadequate testing of existing and additional safeguards and countermeasures.

Some intrusions may not be easily identifiable. It may take the intruders a while to gain access to the system or destroy the system. For example, it took the Hanover Hacker over two years to find a path from Hanover, Germany, to Berkeley, California, to White Sands, New Mexico. As reported by Evans and Morrison, "his intent was to steal military secrets, and he was very determined to succeed." He persisted after many failures to gain access. In two years, his persistence paid off—illegally. He found his way to a military system but was finally caught.

Other intruders have used techniques to disguise their activities. Examples of their avoiding detection include deleting audit trails, doctoring logs and password files, and attaching to files.

While the CIA and other intelligence agencies have taken steps to increase their surveillance of the foreign spy activities on U.S. industries, news media have reported lawsuits undertaken by computer companies against competitors. Alleged charges included theft of confidential business information (such as marketing strategies), information on new product development and planning, trade secrets, and proprietary documents. High-tech theft, conspiracy, and commercial bribery are some of other charges placed against the competitors.

Anthes [6] reports that "frequency of losses due to hacking, bribery, and various kinds of industrial espionage has jumped 323% since 1992," according to the major findings of the 1995 American Society for Industrial Security (ASIS) Property Loss Survey. The average loss is astronomically high. For example, the average loss was $26 million per incident per month.

Anthes quotes Dan T. Swartwood, a coauthor of [7], that "loss of strategic plans, [research and development information], and manufacturing process information accounted for more than 60% of the financial losses." This information is derived from Table 2.1, which lists nine major types of misuse of misappropriated information [7]. The estimates are based on 700 incidents reported by 113 companies.

The U.S. General Accounting Office supports the report's conclusions by reporting that five U.S. allies are spying on U.S. companies. The Computer Emergency Response team at Carnegie Mellon University considers software piracy as "one of the top seven types of computer systems attacks." Anthes refers to the ASIS report that the majority of the incidents (74%) were carried out by the "employees, ex-employees, and other trusted parties." According to Swartwood, there are more and more disgruntled employees due to corporate downsizing.

It is interesting to note that security policies and practices are virtually nonexistent or poor in many companies. This explains why these companies face high exposure to security incidents by insiders. The ASIS survey reports that about 60% of those companies with security policies in place have "security training and awareness programs for employees." ASIS notes that the most common type of attack is for an outsider calling an employee to get confidential information. The outsider uses another name or company and false documents to get the information.

Table 2.1 Misuse of Misappropriated Information 1993–1995

Data	Loss
Strategic plans	$1.4B
Research and development information	$1.35B
Manufacturing processes	$566M
Marketing plans	$460M
Intellectual property	$440M
Financial data	$360M
Merger/acquisition data	$179M
Customer lists	$167M
Personnel plans	$114M
Other	$170M
Total	$5.2B

Anthers mentions that each member of the Congress received a copy of the ASIS report (in April 1996). Hefferman, the other coauthor of the report, thinks the report would help to speed passage of three bills on protection of U.S. trade secrets [7].

One way of determining the impact of industrial espionage is to conduct penetration testing on a periodic basis. For example, Winkler [8] reports his experiences as an industrial spy on assignment from a $5 billion company to simulate an industrial espionage attack against the company for three days. The results show that "penetration test from the inside broke the security of [the]… company." Winkler used five methods of attack: "open-source research, abuse of access, misrepresentation, insider hacking, and internal coordination of external accomplices." For more details, the readers are referred to Winkler's article [8].

2.2 Malicious computer viruses

A computer virus has been defined in different ways. Covington and Downing [9] define a virus as "a computer program that automatically copies itself." The infected programs infect other disks or programs. Those containing malicious routines can disrupt the operations of the system or cause massive shutdown or denial of service to those who depend on the systems for daily business operations and research efforts.

Parker [10] gives a more technical definition of the virus with an explanation of how it works. A computer virus is "a set of computer instructions that propagates copies of versions of itself into computer programs or data when it is executed within unauthorized programs." Unknown to the users, the virus can be introduced through a program or through a Trojan horse. The virus can create new Trojan horses and malicious processes, infecting the entire system to the point of bringing the system to a halt across the geographical boundaries.

According to Parker, a worm attack is "a variation in which an entire program replicates itself throughout a computer or computer network." Although most computer viruses occur in academic institutions, it has been reported that disgruntled employees have introduced viruses into products slated for delivery to customers.

Parker lists "possible indications of a virus infection" (see Figure 2.2):

- The file size may increase when a virus attaches itself to the program or data in the file.

- An unexpected change in the time of the last update of a program or file may indicate a recent unauthorized modification.

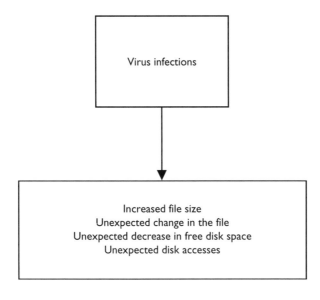

Figure 2.2 A virus infection can be malicious and bring on unexpected results.

- If several executable programs have the same date or time in the last up-date field, they have all been updated together, possibly by a virus.

- A sudden unexpected decrease in free disk space may indicate sabo-tage by a virus attack.

- Unexpected disk accesses, especially in the execution of programs that do not use overlays or large data files, may indicate virus activity.

2.3 Low position on the CMM

The CMM is a capability model that determines how well an organization can develop the software product. It was designed and developed by the Software Engineering Institute at Carnegie Mellon University. The maturity model is divided into five maturity levels:

- *Level 1*: Initial level;
- *Level 2*: Repeatable level;
- *Level 3*: Defined level;
- *Level 4*: Managed level;
- *Level 5*: Optimized level.

Details on maturity models are given in Chapter 6.

The risks to software development projects in a large organization are very high in the initial stage, the lowest position on the CMM. As the organization advances to the next level, more and more risks are reduced to acceptable levels. By the time the organization reaches the optimized level, which is the highest position on the CMM, all risks are theoretically at acceptable levels (see Figure 2.3). To reduce risks in any maturity level, the organization implements all requirements for improvement processes in that maturity level.

According to Yourdan [11], "the success or failure of projects in the level 1 organization is not dependent on the nature of the process being followed…, or even the skill of the managers; it depends entirely on the skill (and perhaps the mood or temperament of the individual(s)) on the project." The organization at this level focuses on personalities, not processes. This level may be a breeding ground for disgruntled employees who may do the following things:

- Leave to join a competing company;
- Become a computer intruder;

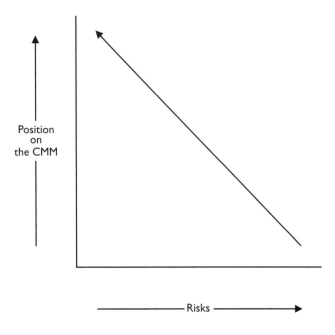

Figure 2.3 The higher position of CMM indicates lower risks to a software
development project.

- Steal confidential business information;
- Become heroes of their own projects;
- Change the specifications in the middle of the project.

If the employees are not disgruntled, they are driven from crisis to crisis or
encounter the last-minute crisis that causes late delivery and cost overruns of the
project. The cost, schedule, and quality performance are unpredictable. Plans
are ad hoc. Resources are always inadequate.

According to Humphrey [12], inadequate project management is another
source of ad hoc conditions. Humphrey reports that a large military software
development project was already very late, and it was determined that small
additions of the functions to the system would meet "within a few months of the
current schedule." However, the added code ended up with 250,000 lines.

Although the project was successfully completed, "the customer lost so
much confidence in the software people that he refused to pay for much of the
work." What went wrong here? The plan was unavailable; project management
processes were inadequate.

According to Humphrey, "organizations at the repeatable process level… face major risks when they are presented with new challenges." Examples of the highest risks at this level are as follows:

- Introduction of immature technology, as well as new tools and methods;
- Inadequate resources and set of specifications;
- Major organizational changes.

To move from the repeatable process level to the defined process level, the organization needs to "establish a process group, establish a development process architecture, and introduce a family of software engineering methods and technologies" [12].

REFERENCES

[1] Evans, Donald L., and J. A. Morrison, "Penetration Testing," in *Handbook of Information Security Management(1995–96 Yearbook)*, F. H. Tipton and Z. G. Ruthberg (eds.), Boston, MA: Auerbach, 1995.

[2] Betts, Mitch, "CIA Steps Up Foreign Technology Watch; Agency Seeks to Prevent Predatory or Subversive Targeting of U.S. Research and Development (Computer Industry)," *ComputerWorld*, Vol. 26, No. 16, April 20, 1992, p. 121.

[3] Carley, William M., "Corporate Targets: As Cold War Fades, Some Nations' Spies Seek Industrial Secrets," *The Wall Street Journal*, June 17, 1991, p. A1.

[4] Greve, Frank, "French Techno-Spies Bugging U. S. Industries," *San Jose Mercury News*, October 21, 1992, p. F1 (2).

[5] Alexander, Michael, "Industrial Espionage with US Runs Rampant," *ComputerWorld*, Vol. 25, No. 9, March 4, 1991, p. 64.

[6] Anthes, Gary H., "Hack attack," *ComputerWorld*, Vol. 30, No. 16, April 15, 1996, p. 81.

[7] Heffernan, Richard J., and Dan T. Swartwood, *Trends in Intellectual Property Loss*, American Society for Industrial Security, Arlington, VA, 1996.

[8] Winkler, Ira, "Assignment: Espionage," *INFOSECURITY*, Vol. 7, No. 3, May/June 1996, pp. 26–28.

[9]   Covington, M., and D. Downing, *Dictionary of Computer Terms,* Third Edition, Hauppauge, NY: Barron's Educational Series, 1992.

[10] Parker, Donn B., "Computer Abuse Methods and Detection," in *Handbook of Information Security Management,* Z. G. Ruthberg and H. F. Tipton (eds.), Boston, MA: Auerbach, 1993.

[11] Yourdan, Edward, *Rise and Resurrection of the American Programmer,* Upper Saddle River, NJ: Yourdan Press, 1995.

[12] Humphrey, Watts S., *Managing the Software Process,* Reading, MA: Addison-Wesley, 1989.

Part II

Part II contains two chapters that cover the discussions on models and practices in software engineering and problems with software metrics. The chapter on software engineering takes the readers to two model types: software maturity and organizational maturity. The next chapter explains why software metrics is important as a measurement of software quality.

Chapter 3

Software engineering

THE CONCEPT OF organizational maturity emerged in early 1990s in the software development industry. It departs from the old concepts of software maturity, which fail to consider the impacts of organizational maturity on software development.

The first model type includes traditional systems analysis techniques. The second model type looks at the SEI Capability Maturity Model (CMM) and the LBMS Process Engineer. The promises and problems of each are considered.

3.1 Software maturity

Software maturity refers to the maturity of the a software development life cycle in developing a product—from concepts to operation. It is based on software engineering principles stating that the models of software development are derived from other engineering activities. Feasibility studies and product design are some of the engineering activity examples. An overview of systems analysis follows.

3.1.1 Traditional systems analysis

This section discusses three types of traditional system analysis:

- Original waterfall;
- Incremental waterfall;
- Spiral waterfall.

Traditional systems analysis started with the waterfall life cycle approach, as developed in the late 1960s and early 1970s. This approach usually involves four steps: requirements analysis and definition, software design, implementation, and testing.

The process begins with requirements analysis and design. When this step is completed, the process moves on to the software design step. The process continues until the project reaches its end.

This approach works primarily if requirements and software design remain unchanged. However, in the real world the requirements and design do change. In addition, errors in requirements and software design emerge at the end of a project. The risks of changing requirements and software design are unmeasurable.

To overcome some limitations of the original waterfall approach, incremental and spiral waterfall approaches (see Figures 3.1 and 3.2) have been considered. According to Edward Yourdan [1], each increment of software development can be managed as a waterfall cycle. Barry Boehm [2] has suggested a series of "increments" in software development. Yourdan refers to DeGrace and Stahl [3] for the following illustration of an incremental life cycle.

In Figure 3.1, the life cycle consists of three main components: system feasibility/validation, software plans and requirements/validation, and the preliminary product design/verification. The product design component is grouped into increments of detail design/verification. Each increment is treated as a waterfall life cycle of the following phases:

1. Detail design;
2. Code/unit test;
3. Integration/product test;

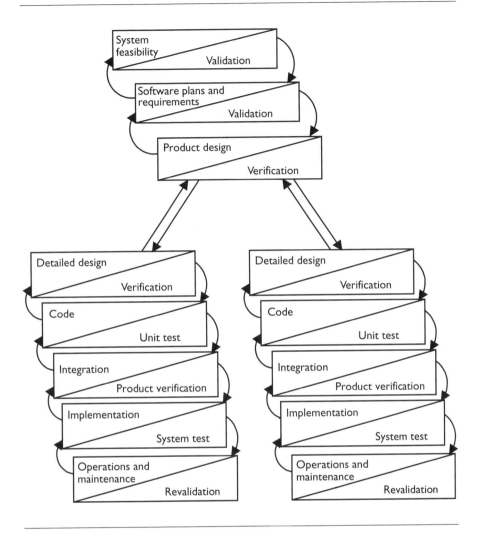

Figure 3.1 The incremental life cycle. (*After:* [1].)

4. Implementation/system test;

5. Operations and maintenance/revalidation.

If an error is found in an increment, the incremental life cycle allows backtracking of the errors in the first previous increment. The backtracking continues until it reaches the increment containing the source of error.

In addition to the series of increments, Barry Boehm has discussed the possibility of developing and managing a software productivity system as a series of "spirals" (within the context of the culture of TRW Defense Systems Group). Unlike the incremental life cycle, the Boehm spiral includes objectives, alternatives, constraints, risk analysis, and prototyping in software development. It identifies and analyzes risks of alternatives for each spiral.

The illustration shows the spiral is divided into four quadrants:

- *Quadrant I*: Determine objectives, alternatives, and constraints.
- *Quadrant II*: Evaluate alternatives, identify, and resolve risks.
- *Quadrant III*: Develop and verify next-level product.
- *Quadrant IV*: Plan next phases.

The horizontal axis divides the spiral into quadrants I and II in the upper portion and quadrants III and IV in the lower portion of the model. It is obvious that the upper portion consists of the objective, alternative, and constraint determination components in quadrant I and the alternative evaluation and risk resolution component in quadrant II, and the lower portion contains the product development and verification component in quadrant III and planning next phases component in quadrant IV. The planning next phase component involves a review of the progress of prior steps and commitment of funds for the next phase.

The spiral divides into four parts. Each is identified with a group function, as follows:

- *Spiral 1*: Concept spiral;
- *Spiral 2*: Simulations spiral;
- *Spiral 3*: Models spiral;
- *Spiral 4*: Benchmarks spiral.

The first spiral is the innermost spiral. Each spiral has its own set of determination, evaluation, development, and planning phases. For example, spiral 2 identifies the risks in alternatives of the requirements validation phase of the life cycle. Spiral 4 identifies the risks of the integration and test alternatives.

The concept spiral starts with the objectives, alternatives, and constraints in the first quadrant. It proceeds to risk analysis of the alternatives and prototype 1 in the second quadrant. The spiral then moves to the concept of operation in the third quadrant. It completes its round with the requirements and life cycle plans in the fourth quadrant.

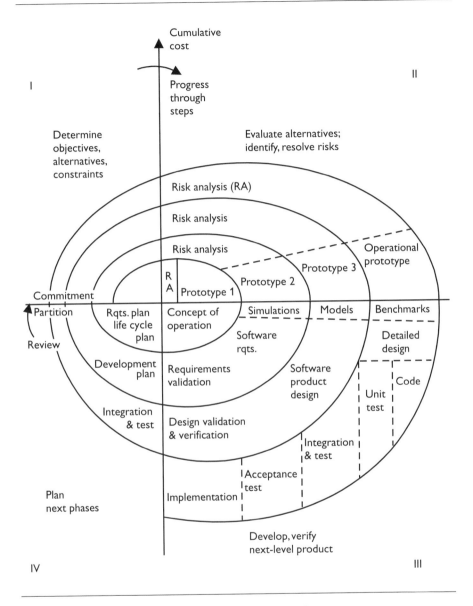

Figure 3.2 The spiral life cycle. (*Source:* [4]. © 1988 IEEE.)

Then, the spiral progresses to the next phase: the simulations spiral. This spiral requires another set of objectives, alternatives, and constraints for the requirements phase. The risks in the requirement alternatives are identified and resolved. The spiral moves to the third quadrant to develop and verify software requirements and requirements validation. It completes with a development plan to prepare for the models spiral.

In this spiral, objectives, alternatives, and constraints of the development phase are determined. This spiral identifies the risks of development alternatives. It proceeds to develop and verify software product design, design validation, and design verification, and then to plan for the benchmarks spiral.

In this final spiral, the risks in integration alternatives are identified. It moves to the next quadrant to develop and verify detailed design, unit test and code, integration and test, acceptance test, and, finally, implementation.

The vertical axis shows the increase in cumulative cost from the implementation component of the benchmarks spiral in quadrant III to the risk component in the outermost spiral. Risk analysis in the innermost spiral costs the least. The costs between the components on each side of the vertical axis are theoretically similar, such as between the development plan component in quadrant IV and the design validation and verification component in quadrant III (see Figure 3.2).

For easier readability, the author has transformed the spiral life cycle illustration into Table 3.1, with a column of quadrants on the left side and a row of spirals at the top. A user feedback component has been added to the end of spiral 4 (to indicate user input into next software releases).

The Boehm spiral model has its limitations. It is difficult to determine from the table the type of risk analysis methodology used for each spiral. Risk analysis is not an exact science, and appears to be a generic term in the second quadrant in all four spirals. Other components are more specific for each spiral in the third and fourth quadrants. For example, concept of operation, software requirements, software product design, and detailed design specifically belong to spirals 1 through 4 in the third quadrant. They are more identifiable than design as the generic word for the third quadrant.

The spiral progresses through steps four times around the quadrants. Similar to the original waterfall model, the spiral completes the current step and proceeds to the next step. However, errors are not detected until the spiral reaches its end. Correcting the errors may be costly because of the many steps involved in backtracking to the source of errors in the spiral.

3.1.2 Systems analysis with CASE tools

This section gives a general discussion of computer-aided software engineering (CASE) and looks at systems analysis with CASE tools as the middle CASE component. CASE is a software tool that provides automated assistance to software development, software maintenance, or project management.

Table 3.1 Viewing Spiral Life Cycle in Table Format

Action	Spiral 1	Spiral 2	Spiral 3	Spiral 4
Quadrant I: Determine objectives, alternatives, and constraints				
Quadrant II: Evaluate alternatives	Risk analysis	Risk analysis	Risk analysis	Risk analysis
Identify and resolve risks	Prototype 1	Prototype 2	Prototype 3	Operational prototype
Quadrant III: Develop and verify next-level product		Simulations	Models	Benchmarks
	Concept of operation	Software requirements	Software product design	Detailed design
		Requirements validation	Design validation and verification	Unit test
				Integration and test
				Acceptance test
				Implementation
Quadrant IV: Plan next phases	Requirements plan; life plan	Development plan	Integration and test	User feedback

After: [4]

Alan S. Fisher [5] shows how CASE methodologies and tools have evolved since 1965, as follows:

- 1965 Structured methodologies;
- 1970 Data modeling techniques;
- 1975 Database 4GLs and database schema design;
- 1980 Design specification software tools;
- 1985 User prototype tools;
- 1990 Code generation tools.

CASE tools automate existing system analysis and design methodologies that have been practiced in various forms since 1970s and 1980s. Some tools are limited in generating codes from specifications. Full automation of code generation directly from specifications remains an academic subject.

The list should be updated to include the reverse engineering tools for 1995. To date, reverse engineering is primarily limited to high-quality programs written in high-level languages such as COBOL, C, and Ada. It is dependent on the strengths of the CASE tool used. The merits of reverse engineering are reflected in the development time it could save. CASE tools have not yet included industry standard risk methodologies.

Today, more and more vendors are offering integrated CASE (I-CASE) tools—either as a software package for a hardware platform or a set of packages for diverse platforms. These tools facilitates the flow of data in an integrated environment.

Breaking down I-CASE into components makes it easier to understand the frame of reference for discussion. According to Michael Lucas Gibson [6], the components contain upper, middle, and lower CASE tools. Upper CASE refers to a component that supports computer-aided planning. Middle CASE refers to a component that support systems analysis and design. Lower CASE refers to a component that supports systems development (e.g., programming). The concept of middle CASE emerged to reserve and expand the concept of upper CASE for corporate planning.

With the advent of middle CASE tools, the waterfall life cycle has become more manageable. Errors can be checked at any point of the cycle. Changes in analysis requirements and definition are possible to correct the problems in the later stages of the cycle, such as software design and specification. CASE tools encourage the use and reuse of libraries of requirements, designs, and specifications to build a software product.

However, Len Fertuck [7], among others, considers the upper CASE as a component on systems analysis and design (see Figure 3.3). For example, Fertuck suggests that standard upper CASE products include analysis and design tools, data modeling tools, and prototyping tools. The first two tools apply to the requirements, analysis, design, and specification stages of the development life cycle. This means when an error, for example, is found in the design or specification stage, the analysis and design tool can be used to trace the error to the requirements stage. When the error is corrected, the tool automatically generates the changed data for the design or specification stage.

Like others, Fertuck acknowledges that lower CASE products include prototyping tools, coding tools, testing tools, and implementation tools. Prototyping tools are useful for the analysis, design, specification, and code and test stages. These tools act as a bridge between the upper and lower CASE products. For example, if an error is found in the test stage, the prototyping tool is used to locate the error in the analysis stage. To backtrack the source of error to the requirements stage, the systems and analysis tool picks up the information from the prototyping tool.

Gibson lists three major benefits of middle CASE, but fails to address the risks associated with this CASE component. The first benefit provides easier methods of changing system design via interactive dialog between the analysts and the users. For example, the analysts consider and analyze the users' needs, and document the analysis with diagrams and dictionary entries. Then, the users make suggestions after reviewing the diagrams and dictionary entries. The analysts consider the suggestions and make appropriate changes to them.

The second benefit facilitates joint applications/design sessions. The end users can quickly influence systems analysis and design. System professionals interact with end users to document requirements at the beginning of development projects. The end users do not wait until the end of the project to provide their feedback to the system professionals.

The third benefit involves prototyping facility, which allows the analysts to simulate the screens early in the analysis and design part of the project. Prototyping serves as the blueprint for building screens to browse, access, and update data.

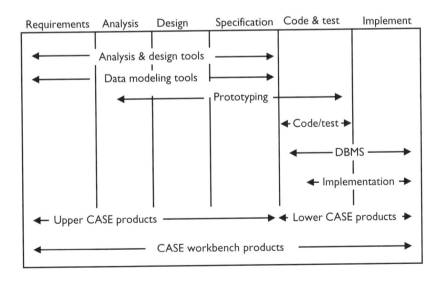

Figure 3.3 Case tools in development life cycle. (*Source:* [7].)

Vessey et al. [8] consider multiuser CASE tools as "collaborative support technologies." They require the collaboration of specialists working together to develop a software product. Vessey's model of a collaborative support environment shows that collaboration technology consists of cooperation technology and coordination technology. Coordination technology is "teamware oriented"; it involves coordination of group activities. Cooperation technology is groupware-oriented; it involves the cooperation of group members to communicate and schedule meeting times about a product.

According to Vessey, an assessment of the cooperation requirements of the CASE tools will require answers to the following questions: Does the tool provide electronic mail facilities? Is it possible to provide anonymous feedback to a team member on his/her work? CASE tools also involve coordination activities in terms of control (namely, access control), information sharing (data sharing, consistency enforcement, and concurrency control) and monitoring (product and user). The following are examples of questions used to assess coordination activities:

Control

Access Control Is it possible to force users to change their passwords periodically? Is it possible to specify read-only passwords for certain parts of the data dictionary? Can one analyst have read-only access to another analyst's work?

Information sharing

Data Sharing Is it possible to simultaneously display the diagrams on all workstations? Is it possible to attach "electronic notes" to objects for all team members to read?

Consistency Enforcement Does the tool automatically notify an analyst whose work might be affected due to a change in the data dictionary? Is it possible to freeze parts of the design work to protect it from changes?

Concurrency Control Is it possible to access the data dictionary concurrently? If concurrent access is controlled by locking, can one query to find who has locked the item of interest?

Monitoring

Product Can the tool flag changes to a data dictionary after a certain date? Can the tool generate reports on every reference to an object in the dictionary?

User For any given user, is it possible to find the most recent login time, date, and session length? For any given user, is it possible to query information on user activity such as the number of changes made at the last login, or data dictionary import/export operations performed on the dictionary?

It is obvious that most questions, more or less, assess risks associated with collaborative and cooperative activities of the CASE tools.

3.2 Organizational maturity

This section looks at the organizational maturity, rather than software maturity, in developing a product in an organization. SEI's Capability Maturity Model (CMM) is chosen from several software engineering models for discussion on organizational maturity of software development processes. The model presents a framework for process management software to automate software development processes. A discussion of the LMBS Process Engineer product suite follows the section on CMM.

3.2.1 SEI's Capability Maturity Model

This section gives a brief history of the CMM and a discussion of the maturity levels of the model. The section also covers an overview of the People Management Capability Maturity Model (PM-CMM) and the Personal Software Process (PSP). It shows how the maturity framework of the CMM is applied to the PM-CMM and PSP.

The concept of organization maturity emerged in early 1990s in the software development industry. It departs from the old concepts of software maturity that fail to consider the impacts of organizational and management styles on software development processes.

Humphrey [9] shows that software engineering is a better method of controlling and managing software development than other attempts at developing software in a chaotic work environment. In 1989, Humphrey presented a model of the Software Engineering Institute's software process maturity model as a framework for evaluating and improving the process of developing software. The model refers to the maturity of a software organization in improving the processes of developing a product (see Figure 3.4). The focus is shifted from fixing problems to preventing them. The maturity is divided into five levels, as follows:

- *Level 1*: Initial process;
- *Level 2*: Repeatable process;
- *Level 3*: Defined process;

- *Level 4*: Managed process;
- *Level 5*: Optimizing process.

The following gives a brief description for each maturity level of the CMM. Most organizations are at level 1 or level 2.

- *Level 1*: Initial process. Software process development at this stage is semichaotic and depends on individual efforts. It provides an opportunity for an automated approach for development and implementation of software process changes.
- *Level 2*: Repeatable process. This stage looks at project management controls for repeating the project successes. A set of predefined process procedures could be used as templates for several approaches to software development. Yourdon [1] has suggested software commitment management, software planning and cost estimation, configuration management, and change control.

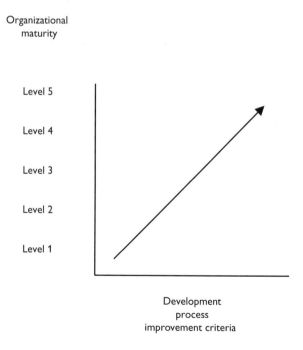

Figure 3.4   Higher maturity level corresponds to improved development processes.

- *Level 3*: Defined process. Process definitions are built from the standardization of development activities in organization-wide software processes. They can be used to tailor the procedures specific to a management or engineering process activity. Yourdon lists the following needed to get to level 3: introduction of formal standards, inspections, formal testing policies, advanced forms of configuration management, formal process models, and establishment of a software engineering process group.

- *Level 4*: Managed process.[1] Detailed quantitative methods, such as data gathering and analyses, are emphasized. They are used to measure the quality of the product and the process by which the product is developed. A comprehensive metrics program would keep track of the defects and the efforts to repair them.

- *Level 5*: Optimized process. The emphasis is placed on the quantitative basis for continued capital investment in process automation and improvement. Innovative process changes and technologies may be used in quantitative feedback.

Martin Thomas [10] points that the CMM indicates "an ordering within process improvement." For example, if an organization is unable to establish effective process management at level 2, the organization will not likely to show any improvements within the process. As a result, the organization will not be able to move to level 3.

One drawback of the CMM is that it emphasizes process, not people. Continued process improvement requires significant changes in the way the development organizations manage people. These are the changes that are not fully accounted for in the CMM. To focus on developing the organization's talent in software and information systems development, PM-CMM was conceived as an adaptation of the CMM. It was felt that as the process of developing people management improves performance, the performance of their teams and projects will improve (see Figure 3.5). Bill Curtis and others [11] show how the four levels of CMM are adapted to people management, as follows:

- The repeatable level focuses on establishing people management practices. They include staffing, performance, training and career, compensation and reward, as well as participatory culture.

- The defined level involves people management planning, knowledge and skills analysis, and competency development. Team building integrates the knowledge and skills needed to accomplish the project tasks.

- The measured level is concerned with establishing a quantitative understanding for the process effectiveness of people management practices. Knowledge, skills, and performance are measured.

- The optimizing level covers the issues of implementing people management continuously. Continuous improvement of knowledge and skills is input from quantitative feedback and adoption of human resources innovation.

Both CMM and PM-CMM are suited for larger organizations that can absorb large overheads. As noted by Humphrey [12], PSP has been developed by the SEI to adapt the principles of software process improvement to small organizations or groups. PSP includes only the CMM items found to be useful for applications at the individual level. It has been found to improve engineers' performance in personal software development process.

Although PSP has a maturity framework of CMM, it is not organized into maturity levels. Instead, PSP progression consists of four components:

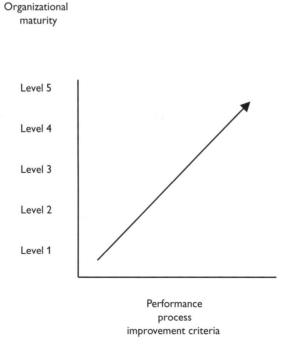

Figure 3.5 Higher maturity level may correspond to improved people performance.

- *PSP0*: The baseline process;
- *PSP1*: The personal planning process;
- *PSP2*: Personal quality management process;
- *PSP3*: A cyclic personal process.

The baseline process establishes a baseline for measuring personal progress in software development. The personal planning process includes size and resource estimations of software development. With the personal quality management process, personal design and code reviews aim to help the engineers to discover defects earlier in their processes.

The cyclic personal process, as described by Humphrey [13], starts with a requirements and planning step for a large program and moves to a high-level design step to partition the program into smaller elements. After this, the elements are developed in PSP cycles. A PSP cycle consists of seven steps: specify code, detailed design and design review, test development and review, implementation and code review, compile, test and reassess, and recycle. The process ends with an integration system test of a product.

The PSP work was conducted at Deimens Corporation Research and the AIS Corporation in Peoria, Illinois. Digital Equipment Corporation and Hewlett Packard Corporation indicated interest in introducing the PSP.

According to Yourdon [1], the following are other drawbacks of the CMM:

1. An organization cannot skip levels; for example, from level 1 to level 4. Much of the transition from one level to the next is cultural. The organization cannot go directly from the semichaotic stage to the stage of formal processes of software development.

2. It may take two or three years to move from one level to the next. On the other hand, mergers or acquisitions could cause the organization to fall back to lower levels. The mergers or acquisitions could result in turnover of critical staff within senior management and technical ranks.

3. Not many organizations are above level 1. As of 1993, the surveys and assessments indicate that 81% of the U. S. sites are at level 1.

4. The organization should not depend on the enterprise-wide introduction of new CASE tools to solve problems at level 1 and level 2. Small-scale, pilot projects on new technologies may continue. The organization must learn to improve development processes.

5. Level 3 is not the place for new software organizations to start. Newly hired people have not worked together as a team.

Three other drawbacks are noted. First, the CMM does not recognize that every project has a unique set of risks. Second, PM-CMM does not consider risks in developing people management. Finally, PSP omits the importance of risk assessment of personal software development process.

3.2.2 LBMS Process Engineer

This section discusses how the CMM provides LBMS, Inc., a maturity level framework for developing Process Engineer (PE) 2.5—a process management software. The product suite helps a development organization automate its attempts to access and improve its capabilities in software development processes.

According to Linda Garrett's product review [14], PE 2.5 is more suited to a large organization that can absorb the overhead costs of automating the model more easily than smaller organizations. It is also adapted to organizations that have proven track records of successes of managing people in a software development workgroup. PE 2.5 assists the organization to start in the initial level of the model. When the organization is ready, PE assists in the move to the next level—one level at a time. PE 2.5 does not allow the organization to skip levels. If the organization falls back by one level (i.e., level 3 to level 2) as a result of a merger or acquisition, PE is useful in returning the organization to a higher level.

PE 2.5 permits project managers to build project plans from methodology templates and automate the tracking and scheduling of application development processes. Users can apply multiple risk analysis and estimating models and customize reports.

PE 2.5 interfaces with a wide range of CASE tools and project scheduling tools, such as Microsoft Project 3.0, Project Workbench 3.0 (Windows) from Applied Business Technology Corp., and Timeline 5.0 for DOS from Symantec Corp. In addition, PE 2.5 can invoke other systems development tools, including LBMS System Engineer CASE tools.

The PE product suite consists of three components: PE/Process Library, PE/Process Engineer, and PE/Process Manager. PE/Process Library is a repository of process templates. Project Managers use PE/Process Engineer, a front-end application, to assess, measure and improve software development processes. PE/Process Manager provides a maintenance tool for the library.

In addition to predefined and customized process templates, the Process Library contains predefined and customized process templates, configurable metric models, and the Process Hyperguide. The templates are used to manage a company's software development activities, such as client/server, rapid delivery, project management, and strategic planning. Managers use metric models to estimate and measure the development process and reconfigure the models in response to changing business requirements.

Process Hyperguide is an online, hypertext reference of work processes and development techniques. The reference contains eight parts: Selecting Adapting, Strategic Planning, Project Management, Client/Server, Rapid Delivery, Classic, Express, and Incremental and Package. It does not reference metric models as one of the main topics.

Process templates are adaptable work breakdown structures (WBS) that provide all the stages, steps, tasks, and end products of a software development process. New or modified templates are built from process kernel modules. PE 2.5 allows the building of a project WBS as a diagram or outline view, and the tool will automatically reconstruct it in the complementary view. Project details are added, such as roles/responsibilities, testing, tools, dependencies, new activities, and new processes. Matrix Editor allows the editing of these details in a matrix form.

PE 2.5^2 provides risk analysis, weighted average, variance, estimate, and function point Albrecht models. Risk analysis assists a project manager to eliminate, reduce, or recognize the impact of risk on the over all project or risk categories (e.g., organizational and technical). It can take place at any point during the project. The relative values of numbers obtained from risk analysis are described as low, moderate, or high risk. Risk analyses are performed by managers who can modify project plans to reflect the results.

Other models look at the quality of the process without consideration for the probable risks to the project. Moreover, PE 2.5, unlike other process management tools, has an expert process analyzer. As the name implies, the analyzer checks the validity of new or modified processes and alerts the user of invalidation.

In PE 2.5, the step-by-step instructions provide onscreen reminders of the sequence of steps to accomplish each function in a project activity. The step-by-step window stays open in front of all PE/Process Engineer or PE/Process Manager screens, providing help for each step. The window can be iconized when not needed. Online guidelines are available to assist the users in selecting and adapting the right process templates.

PE 2.5 divides process management into five levels corresponding to the CMM maturity levels: initial, repeatable, defined, managed, and optimized as described below:

- At the ad hoc level (initial level), PE 2.5 allows an organization to automate the adoption of a methodology in assessing development processes for a project activity. Process success is dependent on individual effort. Formal process for management and development does not exist at this level.

- At the basic control level (repeatable level), PE/Library provides process templates for various approaches to software development. These templates can be reused for other projects. Basic project management controls must be used to enable repetition of project successes via the tracking of schedules, requirements and costs.

- At the process definition level (defined level), PE/Manager tools provide project managers with tools to change the templates or define new process templates in response to changing business requirements. These changes in the software process are documented, standardized, and integrated into organization-wide software processes.

- At the process management level (managed level), PE 2.5 provides configurable metrics and estimating formulas for detailed measurements of the features, facets, and functionalities of the process and the product. The results are collected to compare improvements for both the process and product quality.

- At the process control level (optimized level), the product enables organizations to optimize their software development processes. Quantitative feedback from the process and testing of new ideas and technologies provides continuous process improvements.

Two drawbacks of PE 2.5 are noted. First, the software emphasizes work processes and development techniques; it does not include people management practices. Second, the capability to post electronic notes by remote users is not available.

Notes

1. Level 2 and level 3 organizations measure lines of codes or function points to determine the program size. These organizations also use measurements to count the number of people assigned to a project and the time they spent on the project.

2. PE 2.5.3 provides two metrics models: Contingency and Risk, and Object Based.

References

[1] Yourdon, Edward, *Decline & Fall of the American Programmer*, Englewood Cliffs, NJ: PTR Prentice-Hall, 1993.

[2] Boehm, Barry, "A Spiral Model of Software Development and Enhancement," *Proc. of an Int'l Workshop on the Software Process and Software Environments*, Coto de Caza, Trabuco Canyon, California, 1985.

[3] DeGrace, Peter, and Leslie Hulet Stahl, *Wicked Problems, Righteous Solutions: Catalogue of Modern Software Engineering Paradigms*, Englewood Cliffs, NJ: Yourdon Press/Prentice-Hall, 1990.

[4] Boehm, Barry W., "A Spiral Model of Software Development and Enhancement," *Computer*, May 1988, pp. 61–72.

[5] Fisher, Alan S., *CASE Using Software Development Tools*, Second Edition, New York, NY: John Wiley & Sons, 1991.

[6] Gibson, M. L., "The CASE Philosophy," *BYTE*, Vol. 4, No. 4, April 1989, pp. 209–218.

[7] Fertuck, Len, *Systems Analysis and Design with CASE Tools*, Dubuque, IA: William C. Brown Publishers, 1992.

[8] Vessey, Iris, and V. P. Sravanapudi., "CASE Tools: Collaborative Support Technologies," *Communications of the ACM*, Vol. 35, No. 1, Jan. 1995, pp. 83–94.

[9] Humphrey, Watts S., *Managing the Software Process*, Reading MA: Addison-Wesley, 1990.

[10]   Thomas, Martin, "Top-Down vs. Bottom-Up Process Improvement," *IEEE Software*, Vol. 11, No. 4, July 1994, p.12.

[11]   Curtis, Bill B., W. E. Hefley, and S. M. D. Konard, *People Management Capability Maturity Model, Draft Version 0.2 (for public review)*, Software Engineering Institute, Carnegie Mellon University, Pittsburgh, PA, November 1994.

[12]   Humphrey, Watts S., "The Personal Software Process," *Software Process Newsletter (Software Engineering Technical Newsletter)*, IEEE Computer Society Technical Council on Software Engineering, Vol. 13, No. 1, Sept. 1994.

[13]   Humphrey, Watts S., "The Personal Software Process Paradigm" (Tutorial Presentation), 1994 Software Engineering Process Group National Meeting, Dallas, TX, April 25–28, 1994.

[14]   Garret, Linda, "Product Review: LBMS' Process Engineer 2.5," *Application Development Trends*, Software Productivity Group, Inc., Vol. 1, No. 12, Northboro, MA, Nov. 1994, pp. 75–76.

Chapter 4

Software metrics

SOFTWARE METRICS looks at different approaches in measuring the quality of software development processes and products. One approach is the use of metrics in managing the risks. After a brief discussion of various maturity models, the chapter covers metrics in the Capability Maturity Model (CMM). Then, the chapter proceeds to look at metrics in the Orange Book. It ends with a discussion of other metrics approaches.

4.1 Metrics in risk management

Risk management helps the developers to better protect their projects from disasters and to reduce higher risks to more acceptable levels. To limit the scope of the discussions on risk management in this section, we will give an overview of the following topics:

- Risk exposure and risk reduction leverage;
- Risk impacts.

4.1.1   Risk exposure and risk reduction leverage

Boehm [1] considers that "software risk management is an emerging discipline…" He suggests that its "…objectives are to identify, address, and eliminate software risk items before they become either threats to successful software operation or major sources of software rework."

Boehm suggests the grouping of risk management into two primary steps: risk assessment and risk control. Risk assessment is divided into risk identification, risk analysis, and risk prioritization. Risk control looks at risk management planning, risk resolution, and risk monitoring.

Risk identification contains lists of risk items likely to compromise a project's satisfactory performance. Risk analysis involves the assessment of loss probability with each identified item. Risk prioritization looks at "a prioritized ordering of the risk items identified and analyzed."

Risk management planning involves plans for addressing each risk item, such as cost-benefit analyses of the overall probable loss. Risk resolution looks at how the risk items are to be eliminated or resolved, such as benchmarks. Risk monitoring tracks the project's progress toward "resolving its risk items and toward taking corrective action when appropriate."

Boehm suggests the use of risk exposure (RE) and risk reduction leverage (RRL) as examples of dealing quantitatively with risk assessment and risk prioritization. The quantity RE, sometimes called risks impact, is defined as follows:

$$RE = Prob_{uo} \times Loss_{uo}$$

where $Prob_{uo}$ is the probability of an unsatisfactory outcome and $Loss_{uo}$ is the loss to the parties if the outcome is unsatisfactory.

One example of an unsatisfactory outcome is software error that results in an operational loss. The probability of an operational error is relatively high if the software project shows little verification and validation (V&V). For example, if the software is controlling a nuclear powerplant, the software error could result in a major loss of human life.

The RRL quantity is defined as follows:

$$RRL = (RE_{before} - RE_{after}) / Risk\ Reduction\ Cost$$

where RE_before is the RE before initiating the risk reduction effort and RE_after is the RE afterwards. Thus, RRL is a measure of the relative cost/benefit of performing various candidate risk reduction activities such as V&V and testing.

Let's suppose $1,000K is an estimate of loss as a result of an interface. The probability of introducing the interface error into a software product is 0.3. Let's also suppose that in eliminating the error, the cost of the requirements and design interface checker for the V&V phase is $20K, and the cost of using the interface testing approach is $150K. The introduction of corrective actions will reduce the error probability to 0.1 and 0.05, respectively.

Then, we have the following:

$$\text{RRL (R-D V\&V)} = (\$1000K \times (0.3) - \$1000K \times (0.1)) / \$20K = 10$$

$$\text{RRL (Testing)} = (\$1000K \times (0.3) - \$1000K \times (0.05)) / \$150K = 1.67$$

where K stands for 1,000.

The RRL calculation shows that V&V investment in the early phases of the software life cycle is more cost-effective than the interfacing testing in later phases of the life cycle in reducing the risks.

In the above example, the software interface has been identified as a risk item. Other examples of risk identification items include inadequate staffing, cost overruns, and incorrect schedule estimates.

Example approaches can be found in [2].

4.1.2 Risk impacts

Michael Purser [3] gives a risk analysis procedure for securing data networking and briefly discusses the assessment of risks to some applications in banks and financial institutions, which are heavy users of security services. The procedure is very broad and can be applied to computer systems practices and systems engineering and software development models. The procedure, as described by Purser, could be applied to not only the software assets, but also other assets such as human resources, facilities, and equipment.

Risk analysis contains four major components:

- Identification and valuation of the assets that are to be protected;
- Assessment of the threats to those assets;
- Assessment of the vulnerability of the assets to the threats;
- Assessment of the resultant risk to which the assets are exposed, and of the impact to the organization if the risk becomes a reality.

Risk management is associated with risk analysis. Managing risks aims at reducing the risks at more acceptable levels. They include identifying threats to the assets and monitoring the implementation of additional safeguards and countermeasures. Figure 4.1 shows the selection of a risk analysis method is influenced by three factors. They are identification of security objectives, identification of existing safeguards, and assessment of vulnerabilities.

The risk analysis process starts with assets and needs analysis. For easier reference, the process is arbitrarily divided into five levels. The first-level procedure consists of the following:

- Value the assets that need to be protected (e.g., software).

- Assess the threats to these assets (e.g., software crash).

- Identify existing safeguards and assess vulnerabilities (e.g., system access).

- Identify constraints in implementing possible safeguards (e.g., money, time, legal, and cultural).

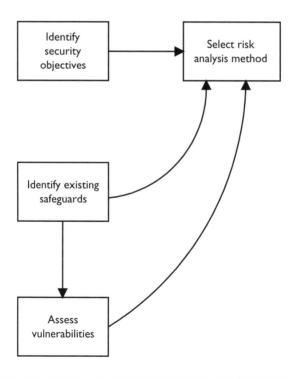

Figure 4.1   Risk analysis method selection. (*Source:* [3].)

In the second level, security objectives associated with these assets are identified. This provides inputs to the third level: determination of risk measures. Other input to this level includes threat assessments, existing safeguard identification, and vulnerability assessments. The measures of risk can be sensitive to the changes in these inputs.

Let's assume the assessments can be adequately controlled. The process moves on to the next level: determination of impact measures. The impacts are measured in monetary terms and are used to compare different risks such as loss of trade secrets, loss of client confidence, or destruction of the hardware.

The last level in the process is the identification and selection of additional safeguards. It receives its inputs primarily from the measures of impacts. Major change in the measures of impacts requires changes in the following:

- Identification of security objectives;
- Identification of the existing safeguards;
- Assessment of threats and vulnerabilities;
- Identification of constraints.

At this point, additional safeguards and countermeasures to remove or contain the risk are considered and their costs of implementing are assessed. Risk impacts are redetermined when serious incidents occur and when changes to the computer assets, such as software revisions or upgrades, are major. Other change examples include tighter budgets and schedule constraints, new threats and vulnerabilities, and higher confidentiality for a computer system.

Obviously, redetermining of risk impacts indicates that the impacts are sensitive to changes and the process is reiterative. The costs of reducing the risks in actual dollar or probabilistic values are reassessed in response to the impact changes. Unfortunately, Purser fails to provide the readers with examples of measuring the process of reassessing risk values and costs for major changes in risk impacts (e.g., changes in software development process).

4.2 Metrics in various maturity models

According to DEF 5169/T1-ImproveIT [4], over 25 maturity models exist. Of these, the following eight models use metrics to measure process and/or productivity of software development life cycle:

- Software Engineering Institute Capability Maturity Model (SEI CMM);

- Scottish Development Agency Software Technology Diagnostic (SDA STD);

- International Standard Organization (ISO) 9000-3;

- ISO Life Cycle Process;

- Software Quality Productivity Analysis (SQPA) at Hewlett Packard;

- Information Technology Infrastructure Library (ITIL);

- Productivity and Quality Enhancement Programme (PEP);

- International Electrotechnical Commission (IEC) 65A.

Of these, three are concerned with risk assessment. They are the SEI CMM, ITIL, and IEC 65A Draft.

The SEI CMM is used both for process assessments and for capability evaluations. Process assessments identify key areas in software development process for improvement. The software capability evaluation (SCE) method focuses on the identification of risks and helps "to set goals and priorities for risk abatement and to assess against these goals." The SEI is funded by the Department of Defense and is located at Carnegie Mellon University in Pennsylvania.

The ITIL consists of a series of guidelines on quality IT services. The source for the ITIL is the Central Computing and Telecommunications Agency (CCTA), which is located in the United Kingdom. Related to the ITIL is the CCTA risk analysis and management method (CRAMM). It is one of the preferred methods of analyzing risks and identifying countermeasures.

IEC, 65A (Secretariat) 94 Draft 1989 "is intended to be used both as a conformance standard and as a development standard." These standards provide assessment guidelines for the safety related software industries, such as transportation, manufacturing, process industries, oil and gas industries, and engineering. Related documents include IEC 880, 1986-Software for Computers in the Safety Systems of Nuclear Power Stations.

Obviously the capability evaluations for the ITIL and IEC, 65A Draft are unavailable. For the CMM, it is important to point out the differences between process improvement and capability evaluations in relation to risk assessment. In process improvement, the CMM is used to analyze the process improvement of each maturity level. The output of feedback includes (besides risks) results, statistics, opportunities, priorities, and "route-map for improvement." On the other hand, risk evaluation is part of a capability evaluation and is used in selecting software development contractors.

Although DEF 5169/T1 does not show that software development capability/review (SDCCR) is involved with the process and productivity improvement processes, it allows the team to analyze the offeror's software development capability and capacity. The deficiency is that there is no model on which to structure the results of the analysis. The source of SDCCR is the Department of the Air Force, HQ Aeronautical Systems Division (AFSC) 1987, ASD Pamphlet 800-5.

Not included in the list of maturity models in the DEF 5129/T1 are the TRILLIUM model, SPICE, and Hewlett-Packard models. The TRILLIUM model is an outgrowth of the CMM. Bell Canada has been working on this model.

Mark C. Paulk and others [5] suggest that "one of the SPICE objectives is to create a way of measuring process capability, while not using a specific approach such as the SEI's maturity levels." Using this approach, maturity levels could consist of sets of process profiles. Paulk points out that "during the development of version 2 of the CMM, one of the technical issues to be decided is whether to re-architect the CMM by layering organizational maturity on top of the SPICE process capability framework."

Perhaps, a reason for the spawn of the CMM-based models is that the SEI's process maturity model suggests that the introduction of the "process" metrics comes toward the end of the process improvement. This is true of the other CMM-based models, such as People Management CMM (SEI) and Security Engineering CMM (NSA). Only the sophisticated and large organizations can afford the overhead to implement a metrics program.

4.3 Metrics in capability maturity model

Metrics in the Software Engineering Institute's Capability Maturity Model (SEI CMM) are basic, process, and optimized. Metrics used are based on the level of maturity of an organization.

According to Yourdan [6], metrics in the level 1 organizations do not exist. The item identified by the Software Engineering Institute as the most common deficiency of level 1 organizations is the inability to estimate software size.

The metrics used in level 2 organizations are "basic" (see Figure 4.2). The level 2 and level 3 organizations, for example, measure lines of code of function points to determine the size of a product as well as the number of people and the number of hours, days, or months consumed by the project. Information derived from the measurements are used to control budgets, schedules, and personnel allocations.

The emphasis in the level 4 organization is on metrics that contribute to the improvement of the quality of both the product and the process by which the

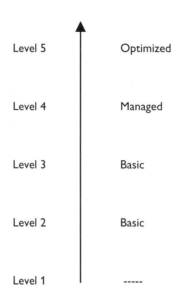

Figure 4.2 Types of metrics in the CMM.

project is built. The "process" metrics look at, for example, the time spent on each of the steps in the design phase and the number of defects found. It also focuses on the time required for each inspection in each step. Measurements include studies of how the numbers vary from project to project, from week to week, and from person to person.

Metrics in the level 5 organizations are used to optimize measurement results. They are derived from continuous process improvement results from quantitative feedback from the process and testing new ideas and technology.

The SEI's process maturity model suggests the introduction of the "process" metrics comes toward the end of the process improvement. This is true of the other CMM-based models, such as People Management CMM (SEI) and Security Engineering CMM (NSA). Only the sophisticated and large organizations can afford the overhead to implement a metrics program.

4.4 Metrics in the Orange Book

The Orange Book is so called because it is the color of the U.S. Government's manual *The Department of Defense Trusted Computer System Evaluation Crite-*

ria.[1] According to Russell [7], the need to quantify security or to measure trust primarily resulted in the development of the U.S. Government's Orange Book.

The book, in part, grew out of a "growing need for standards for the purchase and use of computers by the federal government." It provides security guidelines for the developers, administrators, and managers. The book consists of evaluation criteria for different levels of security and lists requirements for each security level.

The following three basic objectives provided a foundation to build evaluation criteria in the Orange Book:

- Measurement;
- Guidance;
- Acquisition.

The measurement objective provides "users with a metric with which to assess the degree of trust[2] that can be placed in computer systems for the secure processing of classified or other sensitive information." The guidance objective provides manufacturers with guidance on trust requirements for sensitive applications in their trusted commercial products. The acquisition objective provides "a basis for specifying security requirements in acquisition specifications."

The metrics in the Orange Book use four broad hierarchical divisions of security protection to measure trust specifications in descending order:

- *Division D*: Minimal security;
- *Division C*: Discretionary protection;
- *Division B*: Mandatory protection;
- *Division A*: Verified protection.

Division D is the lowest evaluation class on security protections. It is reserved for systems that have been evaluated but have not met the requirements for a higher evaluation class. Obviously, division A is the highest evaluation class, which very few systems have achieved. Each of the four divisions consists of one or more evaluation classes. For example, there is one class in division D; two classes in division C (e.g., C-1, and C-2), three classes in division B (e.g., B-1, B-2, and B-3), and one class in division A. The higher the class in divisions C and B, the more security the division offers.

Class C-2 is also known as the controlled access protection (CAP) class. C-2 users are accountable for login procedures (e.g., authentication), auditing of security-related events (e.g., file attributes, directory rights, and user rights), and object reuse (e.g., clearing of residual data on disks, in memory, and buffers). The users are given or denied access to directories and files. Utilities are required to clear the disks of residual data that could contain sensitive data such as personnel data.

The Orange Book measures trust from two perspectives: security policy and assurance. A security policy specifies the rules for enforcing the system's security features. For example, should a user be allowed to access certain information in a more secure system? Obviously, a highly secure system has more security features than a less secure system.

Assurance is "the trust that can be placed in a system, and the trusted ways the system can be proven to have been developed, tested, documented, maintained, and delivered to a customer." According to the Orange Book, assurance starts at the lowest class with an operable access control mechanism. As assurance progresses to higher level classes, the mechanism becomes more secure. When assurance reaches its highest level, it aims at preventing the user from circumventing the highly secured access control mechanism.

To enforce a security policy, a security model[3] specifies a system's security requirements. The criteria in the Orange Book are based on a formal state-machine model developed by David Bell and Leonard LaPadula in 1973. This model was sponsored by the U.S. Air Force Electronic Systems Division (ESD) and is "the first mathematical model of a multilevel secure computer system."

However, the Orange Book is an ineffective tool for improving the security aspects of the software development process, for the following reasons:

- The Orange Book does not focus on data integrity, as it does on security requirements. Data integrity is an important aspect of software development process.

- The metrics in the book focus on the degree of trust that can be placed in a system—after the implementation of a software product.

- The metrics do not address the issues of measuring the impacts of risk management for each division hierarchy. For example, what are the risks to the system if a software product does not contain an object reuse facility?

- The Bell and LaPadula state-transition model is mathematically formal. The model may not be well-suited to integrate the realistic issues of risk management and the measures of risk impacts.

4.5 Other metrics approaches

This section gives a brief discussion of measurement generations and focuses on the metrics dashboard as an example of the fifth generation. Then, it proceeds to look at object-oriented software metrics.

4.5.1 Measurement dashboard—fifth generation

During the past 40 years, software metrics has evolved through five generations (see Figure 4.3). Measurement dashboard is thought of as an example of the fifth generation.

According to Dr. H. Rubin [8], the first generation, from 1950 to 1970, was the "observable" generation. Measurement categories included level of complexity, GOTOs, and nesting levels. The next generation was called the "code analytic" generation (1970–1978). Examples of categories included complexity, structuredness, and coupling.

In 1978, metrics moved up to the "design analytic" generation. It emphasized categories as function points, graph theoretic, and "bang," a measure of functionality derived from the data-flow diagrams and structure-chart representations of software. In 1984, the emphasis shifted to metrics as feature points, process maturity reliability, failures, and faults.

In about 1990, the "business-directed" generation emerged. It focuses on measures of coverage, technical quality, and other parameters yet to emerge. One example is a measurement "dashboard" (see Figure 4.4).

Dr. H. Rubin proposes ten basic categories of metrics that provide a reasonable "universe for measuring an IS organization, its projects, and applications." These categories are grouped as a measurement "dashboard." The dashboard concept is based on the idea that all organizations must have the available information in the ten basic categories of metrics.

The following is a list of metrics in the measurement dashboard:

- *Productivity metrics*: Rate of delivery of software and the ability to support software.

- *Software metrics*: Technical quality of the software produced and maintained, the functional quality of the context of meeting business needs, and the quality of the software engineering process itself as practiced by the IS organization.

- *Delivery metrics*: Organization's ability to meet time and cost commitments.

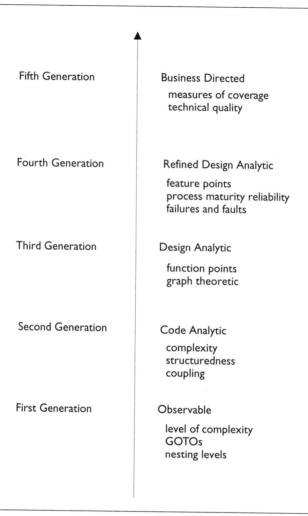

Figure 4.3 Five generations of software metrics.

- *Penetration metrics*: Degree of success of disseminating the tools and techniques.
- *Work profile metrics*: The "shape" of work as it progresses through the life cycle stages in terms of effort and elapsed time.
- *Demand metrics*: Request backlogs and the ability of the organization to service them.
- *Technology assimilation metrics*: Organization's ability to adopt and assimilate promising new software engineering technology.

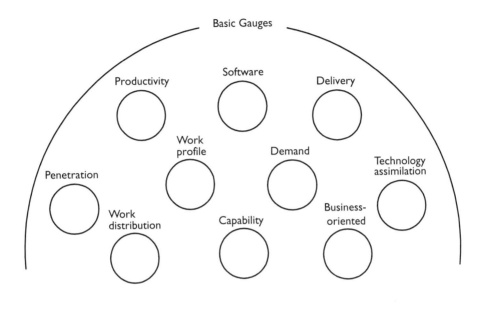

Figure 4.4 This measurement "dashboard" contains ten gauges. (*Source:* [8].)

- *Work distribution metrics*: The balance between maintenance and development.
- *Capability metrics*: Overall ability of the IS organization to manage, measure, and improve itself (software engineering process quality).
- *Business-oriented metrics*: Success criteria used by the business to gauge business performance.

Company focus influences the adjustment of a gauge for each metric. Different audiences (e.g., software organization and project managers) will need different gauges.

4.5.2 Object-oriented software metrics

In 1994, very little work was done on object-oriented (OO) metrics in the industry. Mark Lorenz and Jeff Kidd [9] derived OO metrics from actual project experiences (e.g., C++ and Smalltalk). In academic circles, Kaare Christian [10] considers the theory and evaluation criteria of OO metrics projects at MIT.

In the same year, OOPSLA '94 conducted a workshop on pragmatic and theoretical directions in OO software metrics. The workshop sought to address two issues: (1) tracking progress of OO development activity, and (2) the impact of OO CASE tools on effort estimation and development process. According to OOPSLA '94 Workshop [11], the following areas were covered:

- Measurement and management of the OO analysis and design process;
- Pragmatic application of metrics research projects;
- New research to be initiated to solve measurement and estimation in real-world projects.

OO metrics are useful in interaction and incremental developmental processes. Incremental developmental processes are concerned with new functions (increments) added for the first time to the software development. Interaction developmental processes look at quality aspects of the existing functions (e.g., performance) at various points in software development.

Lorenz and Kidd suggest that software metrics is divided into two categories: project and design. Seven groups exist within each of these categories, as follows:

- Name;
- Meaning;
- Project results;
- Affecting factors;
- Related metrics;
- Thresholds;
- Suggested actions.

Project metrics are used to measure staffing requirements and application sizes. It is also used to measure the progress of completing the system development processes. Unlike design metrics, project metrics do not measure the quality of the software being developed.

The following lists the interdependencies of the design metrics:

- Method size;
- Method intervals;

- Class size;
- Class inheritance;
- Method inheritance;
- Class internals;
- Class externals.

These metrics are based on actual project experiences. They are guidelines that indicate the progress of a project and the quality of the design.

NOTES

1. Department of Defense Trusted Computer System Evaluation Criteria, Department of Defense Standard (DOD 5200.28-STD), Library Number S225.711, December 1985.

2. "Trusted" systems and "secure" systems are not interchangeable. Some systems can be more trusted than others. Not all systems are automatically secure. Evaluation criteria allows users to determine what degree of trust is to be placed in a system. The users can specify what they want to do with the system.

3. For more details on various security models, refer to Morris Gasser's book, *Building a Secure Computer System*.

REFERENCES

[1] Boehm, Barry W., *Software Risk Management*, Los Alamitos, California: IEEE Computer Society Press, 1993.

[2] Boehm, Barry W., *Software Engineering Economics*, Chapter 24, Englewood Cliffs, NJ: Prentice-Hall, 1981.

[3] Purser, Michael, *Secure Data Networking*, Norwood, MA: Artech House, 1993.

[4] Admiral Management Services, Ltd., DEF5169/T1 (ImproveIT), Issue 1.0, Cranfield IT Institute and UK Ministry of Defence, June 1991.

[5] Paulk, Mark C., M. E. Konrad, and S. M. Garcia, "CMM Versus SPICE Architectures," *Software Process Newsletter*, Software Engineering Technical Council, IEEE Computer Society, Vol. 13, No. 3, Spring 1995, pp. 7–11.

[6] Yourdan, Edward, *Decline and Fall of American Programmers*, Englewood Cliffs, NJ: PTR Prentice-Hall, 1993.

[7] Russell, Deborah, and G. T. Gangemi, Sr., *Computer Security Basics*, Sebastopol, CA: O'Reilly & Associates, 1991.

[8] Rubin, Howard, "Measurement: Despite Its Promise, Successful Programs Are Rare," *Application Development Trends*, Vol. 2, No. 1, Jan. 1995, pp. 21–24.

[9] Lorenz, Mark, and J. Kidd, *Objected-Oriented Software Metrics*, Englewood Cliffs, NJ: PTR Prentice-Hall, 1994.

[10] Christian, Kaare, "Making exceptions with C++," *PC Magazine*, Vol. 12, No. 22, Dec. 21, 1993, pp. 311–20.

[11] "OOPSLA '94 Workshop on Pragmatic and Theoretical Directions in Object-Oriented Software Metrics," *Q Methods Report* (Software Engineering Technical Newsletter), IEEE Computer Society Technical Council on Software Engineering, Vol. 13, No. 1, Sept. 1994.

Part III

Part III sets the stage for the next part and presents two chapters on risk analysis and management methodologies. The first chapter covers methodologies used in the security arena. It takes the reader to the next chapter on various maturity models.

Chapter 5

Security

THE PURPOSE OF security is to protect systems from a wide range of threats. The methodologies vary from one industry to another, from one organizational entity to another, from one management group to another, and from one system to another. The purpose of any methodology is to remove or reduce the impacts of the risks of threats to the systems.

Common denominators among the methodologies are assets, threats, risks, vulnerabilities, and safeguards. Their meanings, from security standpoint, are as follows:

- An *asset* is any resource needed to automate a system. Examples include software, hardware, people, buildings, procedures, and files.

- A *threat* is any possible danger or harm to the system. It results in significant damage to or loss of resources, for example, required by the resources need to run the system. The threat is either accidental or deliberate. Examples include industrial espionage, inadequate resources, immature technology, natural disaster, disastrous fire, sabotage, large-scale denial of service, and malicious system intruders.

- A *risk* is the probability that a particular security threat will exploit a particular system vulnerability, according to Deborah Russell et al. [1]. The risks are divided into three to five degrees of probabilities, ranging from "unlikely probable" to "highly probable" that a threat occurrence will result in harm or loss.

- A *vulnerability*, according to Russell, is a weakness in a computer system, or a point where the system is susceptible to attack. The weakness could be exploited to violate system security. Examples include industrial espionage and sabotage vulnerabilities.

- A *safeguard* is any action, device, procedure, or technique to reduce vulnerabilities or to control risks at more acceptable levels. It attempts to protect the asset from harm or danger. Examples include contingency planning and security background of visitors.

A risk analysis [2] starts with the identification and valuation of the assets for a system (see Figure 5.1). The identified assets are most likely to be exposed to a chance of loss or damage without the safeguards to protect the system. Each asset is assigned a reasonable replacement cost.

Next, risk analysis identifies management objectives on security for the system (local or wide area network systems). The objectives include determining the extent of protection needed for the system and the most cost-effective way of providing the needed protection.

Then, the analysis assesses the risks of threats to the assets and determines risk impacts to the assets. After this, the analysis identifies existing safeguards and assesses the vulnerabilities. The analysis proceeds to identify and recommend additional safeguards to protect the assets.

The implementation of the safeguards does not end the process. The process continuously receives the inputs of changes in the management of risk impacts in an interactive fashion. This stage is known as the risk management process. It evaluates the proposals of implementing new or improved safeguards to remove, contain, or reduce new risks.

This chapter focuses on risk analysis and management methodologies.

5.1 Risk analysis methodologies

This section gives the examples of assets, risk impacts of the threats, and replacement costs for both computer and network systems. Then, it looks at

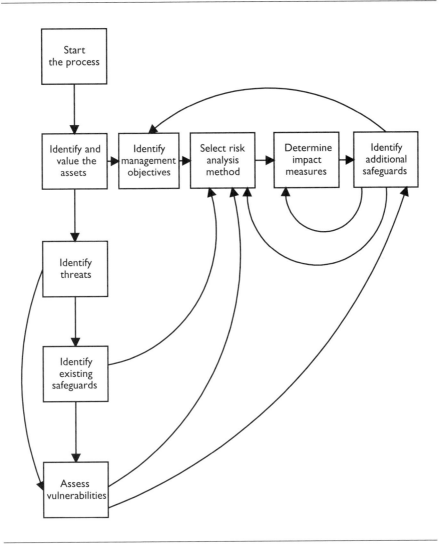

Figure 5.1 Risk analysis process. (*Source:* [2].)

examples of security threats to the assets. The selected threats vary from one system to another.

Risk methods range from very simple to very complex. An example of a simple risk method is a checklist, and, obviously, it takes up the least documentation. A complex risk method requires voluminous documentation with narrative statements. An abbreviated risk method is the middle approach in documenting risk analysis and management. Unlike the checklist, the abbreviated risk method contains abbreviated narrative statements.

These three groups of risk methods are arbitrary (for illustrative purposes). In the real world, the method used to analyze and manage risks may fall somewhere between, for example, the abbreviated and checklist risk methods. The selected method depends not only on the complexity of the system being evaluated for risks, but also on other factors such as depth of user needs, extent of management objectives, and range of organizational goals (see Figure 5.2).

5.1.1 Computer systems

The assets that can be identified and assigned dollar values for a particular computer system are the foundation of a risk analysis. Without the assets, the risk analysis cannot begin. If the assets are not properly identified, a flawed risk analysis will result. If the replacement costs of identified assets are not within an acceptable range, the values are incorrect or misleading and cannot be used as input to an economic value analysis. The following are covered in this section:

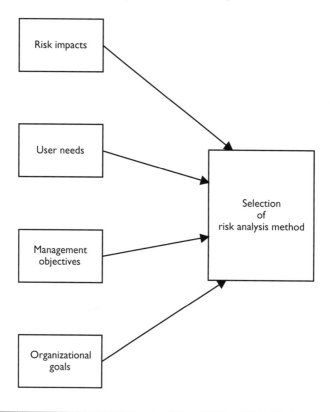

Figure 5.2   Four factors in selecting a risk analysis method.

- Asset groups;
- Asset identification and valuation;
- Threat identification and vulnerability assessment.

Asset groups

This section briefly covers the topics on asset groups to be protected. One of the best approaches to discussing the assets is to take an assumption.

Assume a management objective initially declares seven asset groups for a nondistributed computer system. The asset groups are named hardware, software, human resources, communications, office resources, and data and files. The following are examples of items for each asset category.

- *Hardware assets*, including central processors and peripherals;
- *Software assets*, including operating systems, inhouse applications, system utilities, and commercial programs;
- *Physical assets*, including computer facility, building, and supplies;
- *Human resources assets*, including computer personnel, building personnel, and engineers;
- *Office administration assets*, including inventory records, operational procedures, and contingency planning;
- *Data and files assets*, including data classification;
- *Communications assets*, including network/communications software and switching devices.

The items can be added to the asset categories or removed from the categories for a particular system. In some situations, management can declare an item as an asset. For example, the data classification item in the data and files asset category for one system could be declared as the data classification asset category for another system.

Asset identification and valuation

This section discusses methods of identifying an asset and determining its value. The checklist risk method lists, for example, hardware serial and model numbers, software application version numbers, and manuals. The assets are assigned dollar values to represent the costs of replacing damaged or lost equipment, software, and manuals.

The abbreviated risk method takes a more formal approach to asset identification and valuation. For each asset group, the items are identified with assigned dollar values. This method identifies a risk impact category (e.g., destruction or unauthorized leakage of data) and includes brief analyses to justify replacement costs. The costs are directly or indirectly related to the asset.

For example, the replacement costs of hardware components are directly and indirectly related to the hardware asset. The direct costs include the costs of hardware components. The indirect costs include labor costs of replacing the components. Similarly, the replacement costs of software could be directly and indirectly related to the software asset. The indirect costs considers, at least, (1) how much time the operator or system administrator needs to restore the files and programs, (2) how much time is needed to validate and verify the restored files and programs, and (3) how much time is needed to train a new operator or system administrator.

Threat identification and vulnerability assessment

This section covers sample methods of identifying threats to the systems and assessing vulnerabilities in those systems. The checklist eliminates the need to conduct extensive risk analyses (1) to identify threats, (2) to assess vulnerabilities, and (3) to cost justify existing and additional safeguards.

The abbreviated risk method takes a formal, narrative approach to threat identification, vulnerability assessment, and replacement cost justification. As Russell implies, the following are examples of threat categories:

- Natural disaster;
- Sabotage;
- Fire;
- Unauthorized system access;
- Unauthorized physical access;
- System failure;
- Improper training;
- Theft;
- Massive software crash.

5.1.2 Network systems

The risk analysis process for a nondistributed computer system is similar to the process for a network system. However, the scope of the asset groups, asset identification and valuation, threat identification, and vulnerability assessment for the network system is somewhat broader.

The connection of client workstations to file servers can add new risks and change risk priorities to various assets. If the client workstations are outside of the file server area (e.g., another building or another city), they are considered remote workstations.

The following are covered in this section:

- Asset groups;
- Asset identification and valuation;
- Threat identification and vulnerability assessment.

Asset groups

This section briefly covers the topics on asset groups for a network system. Assume a management objective expands the number of asset groups from seven to eight for a network system. As for the computer system, the first seven asset groups are named hardware, software, physical, human resources, communications, office administration, and data and files. Enter the network asset as the eighth asset group. This asset group contains items unique to a network system.

The following are examples of the items for assets of a network system:

- *Hardware assets*, including file, network, email, database, printer, and application servers;
- *Software assets*, including communications, network, and audit programs;
- *Physical assets*, including server facility, nodes, and supplies;
- *Human resources assets*, including network support group and systems administrators;
- *Office administration assets*, including inventory records and controls, contingency planning, and network operating procedures;
- *Data and files assets*, including data classification and event files;
- *Communications assets*, including network/communications software and switching devices;
- *Network assets*, including data replication, lock, and update mechanisms.

The items can be added to an asset category or removed from the category for a particular system. In some situations, management can declare an item as an asset. For example, the data replication item in the network asset category for one system could be declared as the data replication asset category for another system.

Asset identification and valuation

This section discusses briefly why a checklist risk method is generally not appropriate and covers the topic of an abbreviated risk method for a network system.

A checklist of safeguards is insufficient because the vulnerabilities to identified assets for the network system are not common. The assets as well as vulnerabilities vary from one system to another due to the differences in the system design(s) of network(s). The lack of standard sets of common vulnerabilities makes it necessary to conduct a more formal risk analysis to identify the threats, assess the vulnerabilities, and to cost justify safeguards that may be required.

Similar to the abbreviated risk method for a nondistributed computer system, it identifies asset groups with assigned replacement costs. This method identifies a risk impact category (e.g., destruction, unauthorized leakage of data) and includes brief analyses to justify replacement costs. The costs are directly or indirectly related to the asset.

For example, network devices are directly and indirectly related to the hardware asset. The direct costs include the costs of the components of network devices. The indirect costs include labor costs of replacing the components. Similarly, the replacement costs of software could be directly and indirectly related to the software asset. The indirect costs considers, at least, (1) how much time the operator or system administrator needs to restore the files and programs, (2) how much time is needed to validate and verify the restored files and programs, and (3) how much time is needed to train a new operator or system administrator.

Threat identification and vulnerability assessment

This section covers the topics on threat identification and vulnerability assessment for a network system. To divide threats into categories, the assets must be identified and assigned dollar values to represent replacement costs.

As Russell implies, the following are examples of security threat categories:

- Natural disaster;
- Sabotage;
- Fire;
- Water damage;

- Unauthorized system access;
- Unauthorized physical access;
- Unintentional update error;
- Unauthorized leakage;
- System failure;
- Theft;
- Software crash.

5.2 **Risk management methodologies**

This section discusses the basics of risk management methodologies for computer and network systems. Tom Gilb [3] emphasizes that "risk prevention is more cost effective than risk detection." While full risk protection is not always possible, a methodology can be applied to remove, reduce, or contain the risks.

Small and large organizations perceive differently where the risk management process should begin in a life cycle system or software development. A risk management process can start either at the beginning or at later stages of the cycle. The approach depends on management objectives.

5.2.1 **Computer systems**

This section discusses quantitative methods of managing risks assessed under the abbreviated risk method and a savings justification sheet scenario for non-distributed computer systems.

Quantitative methods

The preferred approaches of quantitative methods are formal mathematics, statistics, and probability. The pros and cons of each method are briefly covered. A discussion follows on why probability is more useful than formal mathematics and statistics.

Formal mathematics is one of the favorite tools for the risk analysis theorists and professional mathematicians in calculating risk impacts. It is used to conceptualize and formalize the quantification of risk impacts. For other risk analysts, formal mathematics can be hard to understand and may not be applicable to real-world situations. Elegant equations with nested summations are not well suited to a large computer or network systems with complex interfaces of assets, threats, and safeguards.

Statistics look at the variations of risk estimates from a norm. A standard deviation is useful in estimating the degree of deviation of the risk estimates. There is one drawback. It is not useful in estimating expected loss of the assets.

Probability is an old science. Simple probability was used in calculating the expected number of heads and tails turned up after flipping coins. Various probability methods have been used in computing the expected results of asset loss.

Simple probability runs from 0 to 1 on a scale. Obviously .002 represents a low probability that there will be a loss of the asset. It is improbable that a risk will occur. A probability of .800 indicates that the expected loss of the asset is very frequent or very high. It is highly probable that the risk will occur. Multiplying a probability to the value of an asset results in a dollar value of the probable loss.

In a more advanced method, weights are applied to the probability values. However, the meaning of the weights may vary from one organization to another and from one system to another. For example, the weighted value of .003 as the low probability for an asset of one system may not have the same significance for the same asset of another system. A management objective may place greater importance on the asset belonging to the first system than on the asset of the second system.

Savings justification sheet scenario

This section covers briefly a scenario on the use of the savings justification sheet. Savings in the example sheet are the differences between the original replacement costs of the assets and the expected asset loss of the same.

Generally, a matrix is used to compute the expected asset loss before and after the implementation of additional safeguards. However, if threat categories are many and most risks are low, it is not cost effective to include all categories in a matrix. It is more practical to compile a list of threat categories whose risks are low. However, due to daily exposure to industrial espionage and threats of competitiveness in the market, the risks of most threat categories would be rated at higher levels.

The matrix should only show the moderate and high risks of threats for specific assets. These threats should be included in a savings justification sheet that shows the savings incurred for adding the safeguards. The savings should result in reducing the risks to more acceptable levels.

In an original risk analysis matrix, moderate and high probability values are applied to the assets for each threat. Methods of determining probability values vary. Whatever the results are, multiply the appropriate probability value (weighted or nonweighted) to the estimated value of the asset to get the expected value of asset loss for each threat. Add the expected values for each asset to obtain asset totals and, then, all values for a grand total.

Then create a revised risk analysis matrix with the same information on asset and threat categories. Change to lower ratings. Compute the expected values for each asset to obtain revised asset totals.

Next, compare the grand totals for the original and revised matrices. If the differences in savings are significant, prepare a savings justification sheet (see Figure 5.3 and Table 5.1) to justify the recommendation of additional safeguards. Changes in management objectives result in reiterative processes of revising a risk analysis matrix and justifying a new return on investments of implementing new safeguards.

To justify the savings, the information should include the following:

- What new safeguards are;
- What the total savings are for adding a safeguard;
- What the costs are for implementing the safeguard;
- What the return on investment is for each safeguard;
- What the impacts are for adding the safeguards to existing safeguards;
- What the priorities are for the new and existing safeguards.

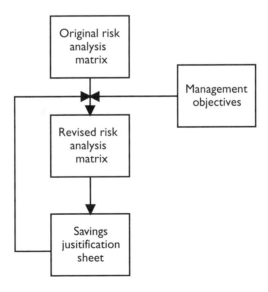

Figure 5.3 Savings justifications are reiterative processes.

Table 5.1 is an example of the savings justification sheet for a computer system:

Table 5.1 The Savings Justification Sheet Gives a Total Return on Investment for a Computer System

Safeguards	Threat categories	Savings	Costs
Password control	Unauthorized disclosure	$10,000	
	Unauthorized system access	$5,000	
Subtotal		$15,000	$200
Contingency plan	System failure	$20,000	
	Unauthorized hardware alteration	$5,000	
Subtotal		$25,000	$350
Summary			
Grand total: $40,000	Grand costs: $550	Total return on investments: 1:73	
Priorities: high for all safeguards		Impacts on other safeguards: none	

5.2.2 Network systems

Risk management methodologies for the computer and network systems are similar. The abbreviated risk method applies to a network system.

Additional safeguards are needed to protect the servers from the risks. The servers are more vulnerable to the risks than the client workstations are. The servers are also more sensitive to changes in system input and management priorities. The measures of risk impacts should be evaluated more frequently to determine if additional safeguards are needed.

One example is the automatic network backup safeguard. The purpose of the safeguard is to record online all transactions in backup media in a storage room located off site. If the same building houses the storage room of backup media and the network system that produces the media, it is not an off-site location.

A second example is the antivirus mechanism safeguard. The purpose of the safeguard is to ensure that software and hardware mechanisms are activated at boot-up time to detect and remove viruses from the system.

In the original risk analysis matrix, probability values are applied to the assets for each threat. Methods of determining probability values vary. Whatever the results are, multiply the appropriate probability value to the estimated value of the asset to obtain the expected loss value of the assets for each threat.

Then, create a revised risk analysis matrix with the same column of threats and rows of assets. Change the rating to low from moderate or high. Compute the expected values for each asset to obtain asset totals, and add all values for a grand total.

Next, compare the grand totals for the original and revised matrices. If the savings are significant, prepare a savings justification sheet (see Table 5.2) to justify savings and costs in implementing additional safeguards and to compute a grand return on investment (ROI). The higher the ratio of ROI, the more cost-effective it is in implementing additional safeguards.

If the grand total of expected asset loss in the original matrix differs significantly from the grand total of the same in the revised matrix, the savings justification sheet should show the following topics:

- What new safeguards are;
- What the total savings are for adding a safeguard;
- What the costs are for implementing the safeguard;
- What the return on investment is for each safeguard;
- What the impacts are for adding the safeguards to existing safeguards;
- What the priorities are for the new and existing safeguards;
- What safeguards are unique to a network system.

Table 5.2 is an example of a savings justification sheet for a network system.

Table 5.2   The Savings Justification Sheet Gives a Total Return on Investment for a Network System

Safeguards	Threat Categories	Savings	Costs
Password control	Unauthorized leakage	$10,000	
	Unauthorized system access	$5,000	
Subtotal		$15,000	$200
Contingency plan	System failure	$20,000	
	Unauthorized hardware alteration	$5,000	
Subtotal		$25,000	$300
Auto network backup	Improper data replication	$12,000	
Subtotal		$12,000	$150
Antivirus mechanisms	Unauthorized software alternation	$10,000	
Subtotal		$10,000	$150
Summary			
Grand total: $62,000	Grand costs: $800	Total return on investment: 1: 78	
Priorities: high for all safeguards		Impacts on other safeguards: none	

REFERENCES

[1]   Russell, Deborah, and G. T. Gengemi, Sr., *Computer Security Books*, Sebastopol, CA: O'Reilly & Associates, 1991.

[2]   Purser, Michael, *Secure Data Networking*, Norwood, MA: Artech House, 1993.

[3]   Gilb, Tom, *Principles of Software Engineering Management* , Chapter 6, Reading, MA: Addison-Wesley, 1988.

Chapter 6

Process maturity models

I N THE EARLY 1990S, the age of organizational maturity for software development processes emerged (see Section 3.2). The focus evolved from software maturity of development processes to how well the organization can improve development processes in a life cycle. During this time, the Software Engineering Institute's Capability Maturity Model (SEI CMM) was in its initial stages. The model incorporated and expanded the concepts of five maturity levels from previous studies at the SEI.

In 1987, Humphrey et al. [1] identified five maturity levels describing the organization's process of developing software. Each maturity level is associated with the level of risk that the software organization is unable to control. The risks are high when a software product is delivered late with cost overruns. Late delivery may be attributed to immature technology, inadequate resources, and inadequate sets of specifications used to develop the product. In addition, software development projects may be inadequately protected from major risks such as industrial and technological espionage.

For several years, the maturity framework of CMM has been applied to the development of the People Management Capability Maturity Model (PM-CMM). The influence of CMM on other maturity models should not be overlooked. The TRILLIUM model grew out of the CMM. There have been discussions on layering organizational maturity of the CMM on top of the Software Process Improvement and Capability Determination (SPICE) process capability framework.

6.1 Risk analysis methods

This section discusses briefly risk analysis methods. Obviously, software maturity and organizational maturity take different approaches in analyzing risk methods. Software maturity looks at the maturity levels of software development life cycle—particularly the identification and analysis stages. Organizational maturity focuses on how well an organization can identify and analyze the risks for all projects.

6.1.1 Software maturity

This section covers the following topics:

- Boehm's risk management tree;
- Risk analysis techniques;
- Risk items;
- Compound risks;
- Spiral model;
- Coordination technology model;
- Risk management deficiencies.

Boehm's risk management tree

The previous chapters have shown that risk analysis methodologies include the processes of identifying, analyzing, and prioritizing risks. According to Boehm, these three processes are grouped under the category of risk assessment.

Boehm's risk management shows that this category is one of the two primary steps of risk management (see Figure 6.1). Risk control, the other primary step, will be discussed in the section on risk management methodologies.

Risk analysis techniques

Boehm suggests the scope of risk identification, risk analysis and risk prioritization, and gives examples of techniques for each (see Figure 6.2). Identifying risk is restricted to those items likely to compromise work efforts in completing the projects. Techniques include checklists, decomposition, comparison with experience, and examination of decision drivers.

Analyzing risks involves assessments of probability of the loss for each risk item, and assessment of compound risks. Techniques include network analysis, decision, trees, cost models, and performance models.

Prioritizing risks looks at the reordering of risk items identified and analyzed. Techniques include risk exposure analysis, Risk Reduction Leverage (RRL) analysis, and Delphi techniques.

Risk items

Risk items are not considered as assets; each item briefly describes the risks to asset(s). Boehm [2] gives the following examples of ten risk items in order of priority:

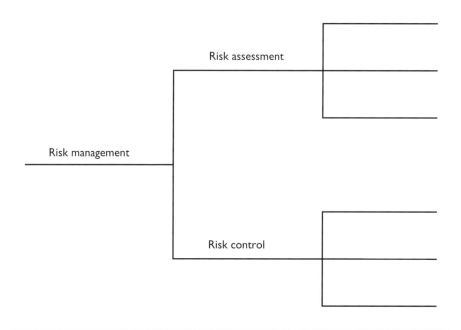

Figure 6.1 Risk management is divided into risk assessment and risk control steps. (*Source:* [3]. © 1989 IEEE.)

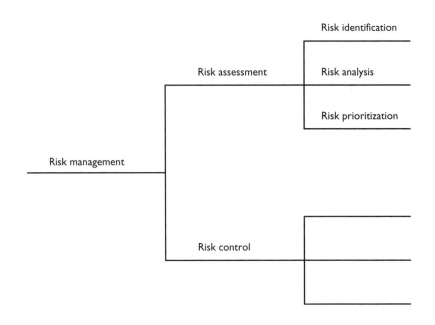

Figure 6.2   Risk assessment is concerned with identification, analysis, and prioritization. (*Source:* [3]. © 1989 IEEE.)

- Personnel shortfalls;
- Unrealistic schedules and budgets;
- Developing the wrong software functions;
- Developing the wrong user interfaces;
- Gold plating;
- Continuing strains of requirement changes;
- Shortfalls in externally furnished components;
- Shortfalls in externally performed tasks;
- Real-time performance shortfalls;
- Straining computer science capabilities.

Compound risks

One of the issues Boehm has raised is whether the risk items can be treated as "independent entities" or as "compound risk items." Sometimes, the "combined" risk exposure is greater than the sum of the individual risk exposures.

The following are some examples:

- Pushing technology on more than one front;
- Pushing technology with key staff shortages;
- Meeting vague user requirements on ambitious schedules;
- Untried hardware with an ambitious schedule;
- Unstable interfaces with an untried subcontractor.

Identifying and assessing compound risk items can be difficult. If at all possible, compound risk items should be reduced to independent entities. If not possible, compound risks should be declared a priority over an array of independent risks.

Spiral model

Boehm's spiral model of the software process provides an example of addressing the risks in a software life cycle (see Figure 6.3). It was developed to overcome problems with risk assessments in the waterfall model and other process models. The Boehm spiral includes objectives, alternatives, constraints, risk analysis, and prototyping in software development. It identifies and analyzes risks of alternatives for each spiral. It was arbitrarily designed to help project managers to incorporate new software technologies, such as rapid prototyping, into the software development life cycle.

Boehm [3,4] suggests ways to tailor a project's management approach to its sources of risk. He describes and compares various software process models, such as build and fix, waterfall, evolutionary development, and transform.

The use of risk analysis in the spiral model determines the ordering of software activities, such as prototyping, requirements specification, simulation, and reuse analysis. The spiral model has applied risk management considerations "to evolve the system's objectives, to evaluate architectural alternatives, to establish increments of system capability, and to employ combinations of prototypes and risk-driven specifications to elaborate the system's definition."

Boehm also suggests bringing the use of the spiral model to the level of maturity of existing process models. He recognizes "the need to bring the processes of risk management, such as risk identification and risk analysis, to a higher level of definition and maturity."

The illustration shows the spiral is divided into four quadrants:

- *Quadrant I*: Determine objectives, alternatives, and constraints.
- *Quadrant II*: Evaluate alternatives, identify and resolve risks.
- *Quadrant III*: Develop and verify next-level product.

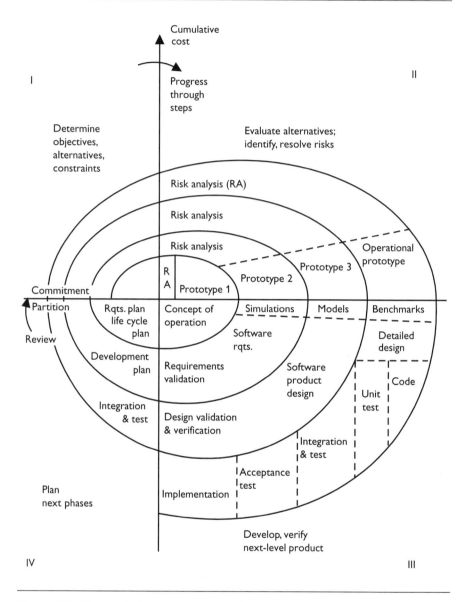

Figure 6.3   The spiral life cycle. (*Source:* [4]. © 1988 IEEE.)

- *Quadrant IV*: Plan next phases.

The spiral divides into four parts. Each is identified with a group function, as follows:

- *Spiral 1*: Concept spiral;
- *Spiral 2*: Simulations spiral;
- *Spiral 3*: Models spiral;
- *Spiral 4*: Benchmarks spiral.

The first spiral is the innermost spiral. Each spiral has its own set of determination, evaluation, development, and planning phases. For example, spiral 2 identifies the risks in alternatives of the requirements validation phase of the life cycle. Spiral 4 identifies the risks of the integration and test alternatives.

The Boehm spiral has its limitations. It is difficult to determine from the illustration the type of risk analysis methodology used for each spiral. Risk analysis is not an exact science and appears to be a generic term in second quadrant in all four spirals. Other components are more specific for each spiral in the third and fourth quadrants. For example, concept of operation, software requirements, software product design, and detailed design specifically belong to spirals 1 through 4 in the third quadrant. They are more identifiable than design as the generic word for the third quadrant.

The spiral model progresses through steps four times around the quadrants. The spiral completes the current step and proceeds to the next step. However, errors are not detected until the spiral reaches its end. Correcting errors may be costly because of the many steps involved in backtracking to the source of errors in the spiral.

Coordination technology model

According to Vessey et al. [5], the coordination technology model involves coordination of group activities in multi-CASE tools. As in Figure 6.4, the coordination technology model is divided into three primary groups: control, information sharing, and monitoring.

The control group is concerned with the issues of access control mechanisms. The information-sharing group considers the issues of data sharing, consistency enforcement, and concurrency control. The monitoring group looks at product and user issues. Some items of the first two groups appear to be risk items that could be identified and analyzed during the software development process of a product. For this reason, the CMM seems like an easier model to work with; it contains a five-step evolutionary paradigm.

Risk management deficiencies

McFarlan [6] suggests that risk assessment helps managers to make better decisions on the outcomes of the projects individually and on a grand scale. He

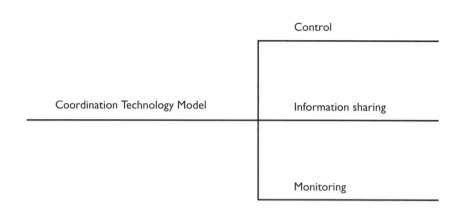

Figure 6.4   The coordination technology model. (*After:* [5].)

presents the following three cases to demonstrate serious deficiencies in risk management.

Case 1

"A major industrial products company discovers one and a half months before the installation date for a computer system that a $15 million effort to convert from one manufacturer to another is in trouble, and installation must be delayed a year. Eighteen months later, the changeover has still not taken place."

Case 2

"A large consumer products company budgets $250,000 for a new computer-based personnel information system to be ready in nine months. Two years later, $2.5 million has been spent, and an estimated $3.6 million more is needed to complete the job. The company has to stop the project."

Case 3

"A sizable financial institution slips $1.5 million over budget and 12 months behind on the development of programs for a new financial systems package, vital for the day-to-day functioning of one of its major operating groups. Once the system is finally installed, average transaction response times are much longer than expected."

McFarlan believes that the first two are the result of the failure to assess individual risks in a project and to consider the aggregate risks of the portfolio of projects. The third case is the failure to recognize that different projects need different management objectives and approaches to managing the risks.

However, risk assessment techniques from software maturity perspectives will not always prevent the failure to identify and analyze most risks inherent in the software development process. Software maturity focuses on the maturity of risk assessment processes. Unlike organizational maturity, it does not consider how well an organization can identify and analyze the risks in the software development process life cycle.

Risk assessment techniques from organizational maturity perspectives will increase the chances of a project's success. Organizational maturity looks at how well the organization can handle the process of risk identification and analysis for all software development projects across the organization.

6.1.2 Organizational maturity

This section covers the following topics:

- The CMM and related models;
- The CMM versus SPICE;
- TRILLIUM;
- SEI Risk Management Paradigm;
- Automated CMM framework;
- Automated risk analysis.

The CMM and related models

The SEI built the CMM to improve the delivery and quality of software products. The CMM was conceived in the age of organizational maturity in the early 1990s.

The model's aim was to focus more on assessing and improving a software development organization's capabilities in each maturity stage. The CMM consists of five maturity levels: initial, repeatable, defined, managed, and optimized. Each level is briefly described as follows:

- *Level 1*: Initial process. Software process development at this stage is semichaotic and depends on individual efforts. It provides an opportunity for an automated approach for the development and implementation of software process changes.
- *Level 2*: Repeatable process. This stage looks at project management controls for repeating the project successes. A set of predefined tasks and processes should be defined well enough to allow a project manager to predict the results of software development projects with reasonable accuracy. Examples include commitments, change controls, costs, and project tracking.

- *Level 3*: Defined process. Process definitions are built from the standardization of development activities in organization-wide software processes. They can be tailored to a management or engineering process activity. The processes allow one to predict the effect of implementing new technologies. At this level, standards need to be formalized, inspections need to be conducted, formal testing policies need to be established, and process models need to be formalized. In addition, a software engineering process group needs to be established.

- *Level 4*: Managed process. Detailed quantitative methods, such as data gathering and analyses, are emphasized. They are used to measure the quality of the product and the process by which the product is developed. A comprehensive metrics program would keep track of the defects and the efforts to repair them.

- *Level 5*: Optimized process. The emphasis is placed on the quantitative basis for continued capital investment in process automation and improvement. Innovative process changes and technologies may be used in quantitative feedback.

Most software development organizations in the United States are below level 3. Williamson [7] reports that "in a September 1995 SEI assessment of 440 organizations, over 70 percent were still at level one." Only 1% reached level 4 and one organization successfully advanced to level 5. However, this does not take into account more than a thousand other assessments that have taken place but were not included in the September 1995 SEI assessment evaluations.

The organization must show all process improvements required of a maturity level before proceeding to the next level. It is important to identify and assess risks in the early maturity levels. Theoretically, the higher the maturity level is, the lower the risks are to the development processes. However the CMM may not address the risks unique to a project or even an organization. It is more suited for a large organization that can more readily absorb large overhead in assessing a maturity level than the smaller organization can. Assessment procedures include an evaluation assessment instrument (e.g., a formal questionnaire) that is used to elicit responses in several interviews on risk identification and analysis.

One drawback of the CMM is that it emphasizes process, not people. Continued process improvements requires significant changes in the way the development organizations manage people. These are the changes that are not fully accounted for in the CMM. People are important. Disgruntled employees and individuals are a threat to software development projects.

To focus on developing the organization's talent in software and information systems development, PM-CMM was conceived as an adaptation of the CMM. It was felt that as the process of developing people management improves performance, the performance of their teams and projects would improve (see Figure 6.5). Bill Curtis and others [8] shows how the four levels of CMM are adapted to people management, as follows:

- *Level 2*: This repeatable level focuses on establishing people management practices. They include staffing, performance, training and career, compensation and reward, as well as participatory culture.

- *Level 3*: This defined level involves people management planning, knowledge and skills analysis, and competency development. Team building integrates the knowledge and skills needed to accomplish the project tasks.

- *Level 4*: This measured level is concerned with establishing a quantitative understanding for the process effectiveness of people management practices. Knowledge, skills, and performance are measured.

- *Level 5*: This optimizing level covers the issues of implementing people management continuously. Continuous improvement of knowledge and skills receives its input from quantitative feedback and adoption of human resources innovation.

Metrics in the CMM and PM-CMM are basic, process, and optimized. Metrics used are based on the level of maturity of an organization. Details on metrics used are discussed in Section 6.2.2 on organizational maturity.

Regardless of the variations of the CMM, it is better than the ISO-9000 approach (which was not originally developed for software processes). According to Yourdan [9], ISO-9000 certification is approximately equal on level 3 of the SEI scale. However, the certification is binary; the organization is certified or not certified. On the other hand, the CMM takes the five-level evolutionary approach. Noncertification may make it difficult for a certain organization's efforts to improve. With the CMM, the organization would know which key areas to improve in order to move up to level 2 and then to level 3.

The CMM versus SPICE

Paulk and others [10] suggest that one of the SPICE objectives is to create a way of measuring process capability while not using a specific approach such as the SEI's maturity levels. SPICE looks at a process measure rather than an organi-

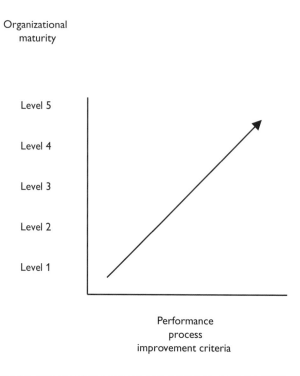

Figure 6.5 A higher maturity level may correspond to improved people performance.

zation measure. While developing version 2 of the CMM, a technical issue was brought up on "whether to rearchitect the CMM by layering organizational maturity on top of the SPICE process capability framework."

The ISO has been developing standards on software process assessment under SPICE. Baseline Practice Guide (BPG) is one of the SPICE products comprising the proposed software process assessment standard. The BPG is the SPICE equivalent of the SEI's CMM.

The BPG categorizes processes into five process categories:

- Customer-supplier;
- Engineering;
- Project;
- Support;
- Organization.

Paulk et al. [10] point out that there are six capability levels in the BPG:

- *Not performed* level (0);
- *Performed informally* level (1);
- *Planned and tracked* level (2);
- *Well-defined* level (3);
- *Quantitatively controlled* level (4);
- *Continuously improving* level (5);

BPG common features are clustered according to capability levels. For example, the common features at capability level 2, *planned and tracked,* are

- Planning performance;
- Disciplined performance;
- Verifying performance;
- Tracking performance.

The advantages and disadvantages of the CMM and SPICE are noted. One advantage of the BPG architecture is that it measures the evolution of each process. The aspects of each process can be reviewed independently of other processes. On the other hand, the key process areas in the CMM reside at a single maturity level. Matured processes are described in different key process areas at different levels. The following is an example of the evolution of the processes in the CMM:

- *Level 2*: Software project planning and software project tracking and oversight;
- *Level 3*: Software management;
- *Level 4*: Quantitative process management;
- *Level 5*: Process change management.

One disadvantage of the BPG architecture is that less important process issues can take the stage over the more important process issues. One disadvantage of the CMM architecture is that some important processes might be lost when they are not a focus of a particular maturity level.

To overcome the disadvantages, the maturity levels in the CMM can be layered on top of the BPG capability levels. The repeatable process (2) in the CMM is layered on top of project and support process categories with process capabilities 0, 1, and 2. The defined process (3) is layered on top of engineering, project, support, and organization process categories with a range of process capabilities of 0 through 3. For example, The CMM emphasizes project management at level 2 and defers organizational and engineering processes to level 3. However, it would make more sense to recognize the fact engineering processes are performed at level 2 at the project level.

The managed level (4) covers partially the customer-supplier process category and fully the engineering, project, support and organization process categories with process capabilities 0 through 4. The optimizing level (5) also covers partially the supplier-process category and fully the engineering, project, support and organization process categories only for process capability 5.

TRILLIUM

TRILLIUM stands for Telecom Software Product Development Capability Assessment Model and is a joint effort of Bell Canada, Bell Northern Research (Canada) and Northern Telecom (Canada). The model is used to assess the capabilities of telecommunications system suppliers. According to Andrew and others [11], TRILLIUM is derived from the CMM and maps levels of the CMM into "a combination of the original CMM and various development standards including ISO 9001 and the IEEE Software Engineering Standards." Unlike the CMM, each maturity level of TRILLIUM is grouped into exactly ten factors, which can be further divided into several attributes.

SEI risk management paradigm

According to Vacca [12], software development activities must be planned, managed, and evaluated to improve the quality of software products and to increase work productivity. However, there are risks inherent in the development process. The risks, if not properly managed and evaluated, could compromise the project's expected success.

The SEI has shown it is possible to adapt risk management within the framework of the CMM. It developed a software risk management paradigm consisting of five components: identify, analyze, plan, track, and control. Each component receives its feedback from the previous component.

Risk identification and analysis is a repeatable process. Basic management controls (or objectives) target toward the repetition of the successes of identifying and analyzing management and technical risks to software development process. This increases the probability of delivering a product within budget and on schedule—not for one project but across the organization for all projects. Higher probabilities are achieved through the tracking and reporting of implementation costs, project schedules, and risk assessment requirements.

At the repeatable process level, predefined templates are used to identify and analyze risks to the software development process. The templates could consist of, for example, four different approaches or techniques of risk identification and analysis.

The selection of an approach depends on the complexity of the development process, the time to complete the process, the size of budget, and the complexity of compound and independent risks. One approach example consists of an evaluation assessment instrument (e.g., a formal questionnaire) that is used to elicit responses in several interviews on risk identification and analysis.

After management objectives have established standards on predefined templates, they should allow project leaders to modify the existing templates or define new templates specific to an organization. New risks may have emerged and some existing risks may have become obsolete for a specific organization. As a result, templates need to be modified or created for the organization. This should result in organizational and methodological improvements in risk assessment processes.

One example is the establishment of procedures on adapting or modifying predefined templates or creating new ones in response to risk requirement changes. A template could be in the form of a series of evaluation assessment worksheets for each risk item and threat could be developed from questionnaires. Another example is the establishment of risk assessment groups that would focus on the adequacy of implementing the process of various risk assessment methodologies.

The organizations that show significant organizational and methodological improvements would proceed to the next higher maturity level: the defined process. At this stage, management activities in the risk management process are documented, standardized, and integrated into organization-wide risk management processes.

Automated CMM framework

The CMM provides a framework for assessing and improving the way organizations develop software. LBMS, Inc., Houston, developed its Process Engineer (PE) product to help development organizations automate their attempts to assess and improve their processes for developing software.

PE is more suited to a large organization that can absorb the overhead costs of automating the model more easily than smaller organizations. The software allows project managers to build project plans from methodology templates and automate the tracking and scheduling of application development processes. Users can apply estimating models and customize reports.

PE provides risk analysis, weighted average, variance, estimate, and function point Albrecht and Markel models. According to Garrett [13], risk analysis assists in improving the management of risks to the development process. Other models look at the quality of the process without consideration for the risks to the process.

PE allows the users to change the algorithms and modeling of risk analysis in response to changing business requirements, management objectives. and the impacts of analysis results. Garrett suggests that PE supports all five levels of the CMM: initial, repeatable, defined, managed, and optimized.

Automated risk analysis

The purpose of automated risk analysis in PE is to identify and quantify areas of uncertainty during an organization's assessment and improvement of software development projects. The relative values of risk analysis indicate whether the overall project is of low, moderate, high, or extreme risk.

Risk analysis is a structured attempt to identify and analyze areas of uncertainty throughout the life of a project according to its potential threat. Anticipation of threats will allow alternatives of reducing the risks to more acceptable levels.

Risk analysis can take place at any point during the project, regardless of the maturity level the project has achieved. However, the earlier in the project, the more useful the results. These results could serve as inputs into risk analysis on later maturity stages.

The following are examples of categories so identified, each of which might contain some degree of uncertainty and have a potential impact on a group's success in delivering the project on time, within budget, and within adequate resources:

- Plan;
- Organizational;
- Technical;
- External dependencies.

6.2 Risk management methodologies

This section discusses briefly risk management methods. Software maturity and organization maturity differ in the way the risks are managed.

6.2.1 Software maturity

This section covers the following topics:

- Boehm's risk management tree;
- Risk management techniques;
- Coordination technology model.

Boehm's risk management tree

As mentioned in Section 6.1, risk management consists of two primary groups: risk assessment and risk control. Risk control involves risk management planning, risk resolution, and risk monitoring (see Figure 6.6).

Planning risk management involves plans for addressing each risk item or a set of risk items for the overall project. Typical techniques include checklists of resolution techniques, cost-benefit analysis, and statistical decision analysis of the relative cost and effectiveness of alternative risk resolution techniques.

Resolving risks aims at removing the risks or relaxing requirements. Typical techniques include prototypes, simulations, benchmarks, mission analyses, key personnel agreements, design-to-cost approaches, and incremental development.

Monitoring risks involves tracking the project's progress toward resolving its risk items and toward taking corrective action when appropriate. Typical

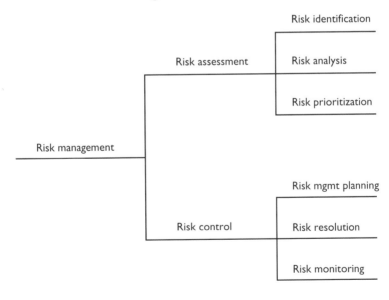

Figure 6.6 Risk control is concerned with management planning, resolution, and monitoring. (*Source:* [3]. © IEEE 1989.)

techniques include risk management plan milestone tracking and a periodic or milestone project review.

Risk management techniques

Boehm [2] gives examples of risk management techniques for the following risk categories:

- Personnel shortfalls;
- Unrealistic schedules and budgets;
- Requirement risks;
- Shortfalls in external components and tasks;
- Straining computer science capabilities.

For each of the following ten risk categories, risk resolution techniques are listed. Further details on the techniques are provided in Boehm's book.

The *personnel shortfalls* item is the top priority. A good staff with key skills is needed to start a software development project. To reduce the risks of this item, the following techniques are recommended:

- Staffing with top talent, job matching, and team building;
- Key personnel agreements and training;
- Staffing and prescheduling key people.

Most risks that cause a project's schedule and budget difficulties are specific to a project. The following techniques are useful in lowering the risks of the *unrealistic schedules and budgets* item to more acceptable levels:

- Detailed multisource cost and schedule estimation;
- Design to cost (fixed) and incremental development;
- Software reuse and requirements scrubbing.

User's requirements not fully understood may increase the risks of the *developing the wrong software functions*. This risk item can be reduced with the following:

- Organizational analysis, mission analysis, and user surveys;
- Prototyping and early user's manuals.

In projects where software functionality is considered inadequate, unfriendly user interfaces may occur. The following techniques of minimizing the risks inherent in the *developing the wrong user interfaces* item are recommended:

- Prototyping, scenarios, and task analysis;
- User characterization.

The *gold plating* item refers to the process of adding complex but marginally useful features to software products. The following are some techniques of resolving or reducing this risk:

- Requirements scrubbing and prototyping;
- Cost-benefit analysis and design to cost.

Some software requirements changes are essential. Risks occur when projects underestimate the impacts of requirements changes on the development life cycle. The risks associated with the *continuing stream of requirements changes* item can be brought down to more acceptable levels with the following:

- High change threshold;
- Information hiding (on requirement changes);
- Incremental development.

Examples of external components as sources of risk are the customer-furnished components mismatched with those of a new application. Reducing the risks of the *shortfalls in externally furnished components* item are accomplished with the following:

- Benchmarking, inspections, and reference checking;[1]
- Compatibility analysis.

Examples of external tasks as sources of risks include legal reviews and security clearances, and customers' unrealistic expectations of a software development specification. Techniques are available for reducing the risks of the *shortfalls in externally performed tasks* item, such as the following:

- Reference checking and team building;
- Competitive design on prototyping.

A variety of techniques are available to reduce the risk that a software system's performance will be inadequate or frequently downgraded. The techniques for reducing the risks of the *real-time performance shortfalls* item include the following:

- Simulation, benchmarking, and modeling;
- Prototyping, instrumentation, and tuning.

Other sources of risks are the projects that neglect to consider if limited computer resources can meet software requirements. Techniques for reducing the *straining computer science capabilities* item include the following:

- Technical analysis and costs-benefit analysis;
- Prototyping and reference checking.

Coordination technology model

Vessey et al. [5] include *monitoring* as the third primary group in the coordination technology model. This group is limited to products and users. It does not address the issues of monitoring the risks in the processes of access control and information sharing, particularly data-sharing consistency enforcement and concurrency control. It is concerned with the issues of monitoring a software product after it is developed.

However, the issues of access control and information sharing could be adapted to identify and analyze the risks in a development life cycle. Responses to a questionnaire could be used to develop techniques such as planning risk management, resolving risks, and monitoring risks

6.2.2 **Organizational maturity**

This section covers the following topics:

- Metrics in the CMM;
- The SEI algorithm;
- Human resources;
- Risk management issues;
- CMM case studies;
- Cognitive bias.

Metrics in the CMM

According to Yourdan [14], metrics in the level 1 organization do not exist. The item identified by the Software Engineering Institute as the most common deficiency of level 1 organizations is the inability to estimate software size.

The metrics used in level 2 organizations are "basic" (see Figure 6.7). The level 2 and level 3 organizations, for example, measure lines of code of function points to determine the size of a product as well as the number of people and the number of hours, days, or months consumed by the project. Information derived from the measurements are used to control budgets, schedules, and personnel allocations.

The emphasis in the level 4 organization is on metrics that contribute to the improvement of the quality of both the product and the process by which the project is built. The process metrics look at, for example, the time spent on each of the steps of the design phase and the number of defects found. It also focuses on the time required for each of the inspections in each of the steps. Measurements include studies of how the numbers vary from project to project, from week to week, and from person to person.

Metrics in the level 5 organizations are used to optimize measurement results. They are derived from continuous process improvement results from a quantitative feedback from the process and testing new ideas and technology.

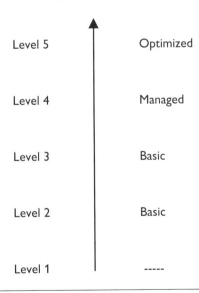

Level 5	Optimized
Level 4	Managed
Level 3	Basic
Level 2	Basic
Level 1	-----

Figure 6.7 Types of metrics in the CMM.

The SEI's process maturity model suggests that the introduction of the process metrics comes toward the end of the process improvement process. This is true of other CMM-based models, such as People Management CMM (SEI) and Security Engineering CMM (NSA). Only the sophisticated and large organizations can afford the overhead to implement a metrics program.

The SEI algorithm

Theoretically, each maturity level in the CMM indicates the level of risk. The lower the maturity level is, the greater or more the risks are to the software development processes (see Figure 6.8). The higher the maturity level is, the better the chance is to improve the process maturity. Improvement is accomplished by introducing, in sequential steps (see Figure 6.9), techniques and methods such as configuration management, project management, explicit process definition, quality control, and product evaluation. At level 5, software process is continuously improved. The data is reassessed as to the impacts of introducing new technologies on the process across the organization.

The SEI uses questionnaires to elicit responses on process improvement for each maturity level. The higher the maturity level is, the fewer the number of

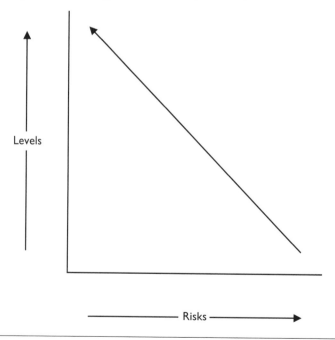

Figure 6.8   The CMM theoretically implies that the higher the maturity level is, the lower the risks are.

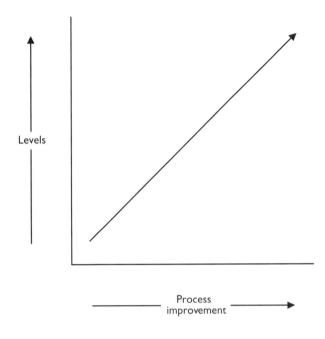

Figure 6.9   Higher maturity levels imply a greater degree of process improvement.

questions. This is in contrast to security requirements for the detailed information needed to assess and manage risks. The larger and more complex software development processes are, the more complex risk analysis and management processes become. Complex development processes require complex computational evaluations to determine expected asset loss and probable savings with current and additional safeguards.

An organization cannot proceed to a higher maturity level in the CMM without completing all process improvement criteria at the current maturity level. This also applies to the organization that has completed some aspects of process improvement at the higher maturity level, but not all of the processes at the current level.

For example, according to Hasse et al. [15], an organization can be rated a level 1 for efficient project management and level 3 for efficient design methodology. However, the CMM algorithm would assign the organization an overall level 1. The organization must meet process improvement criteria for level 2 before proceeding to level 3. According to the SEI algorithm, all risks must be resolved at a current maturity level before the organization proceeds to obtain a rating for the next higher level.

Human resources

Bandinelli [16] refers to the research by Johnson and Brodman [17] on the applicability of the SEI CMM to small and medium-sized organizations. For example, small organizations find it physically impossible to establish groups such as a software engineering process group (SEPG). These organizations may not have the staff to support process improvement. Bandinelli mentions that the "SEI CMM suggests 2% of software professionals for the SEPG staff." In a small organization, 2% may represent a small fraction of a person.

The inability of the small or medium-sized organization to provide human resources to support improvement initiative poses greater risks to software development processes. The SEI's Software Risk Management Paradigm may not be applicable to small or medium-sized organizations that cannot provide human resources to assess and manage risks according to the SEI algorithm. The paradigm is more suitable to larger organizations that can absorb the overhead costs of improving CMM-based development processes. The concepts of repeatable, defined, managed, and optimized processes of risk management are borrowed from the CMM.

Risk management issues

A possible problem with the use of questionnaires (e.g., the CMM) to assess risks is that each software development may have a set of risks unique to that project. Questionnaires may be suitable to one project, but not to another. Worksheets and other more formal assessment evaluation instruments should be developed and established for each project. Risk assessment documentation should be broader in scope and in depth to allow the flexibility of choosing a risk management method for a project. The method, for example, could range from "abbreviated format" to "comprehensive collection and analysis of data."

The SEI questionnaires limit the CMM to identifying, analyzing, defining, managing, and optimizing technical areas of process improvement across the organization. The model looks at how well an organization can improve the processes of developing a software product and reduce risks to the processes. The higher the maturity level is, the lower the risk levels become. However, the model does not aid in identifying, analyzing, defining, managing, and optimizing risks unique to organizational processes that could be improved.

For some organizations, the CMM implementation of a process improvement initiative may require the reorganization of a software development company (e.g., department mergers and human resource hiring). Any risk management method targeted for integration with the CMM will need to be reconsidered. For example, a reorganization may require a different risk management method and a different management objective for implementing the method. New risks, new development processes, and new technology requirements unique to each project may have emerged during the reorganization.

Another risk management issue is the time to manage risks after the risks are identified and assessed. The length of time to lower the risks to more acceptable levels for each maturity level may be unrealistic. For example, it may take an organization five years to proceed from level 1 to level 2, or from level 2 to level 3. From a security standpoint, five years to lower the risks may not be economically feasible. A natural disaster could occur at the organization during the improvement processes of software development. Recovery from the disaster is more expensive when recovery plans are insufficient or nonexistent than when those plans are implemented and managed during early stages of each maturity level.

CMM case studies

Bandinelli et al. [16] give two examples of industrial experiences to increase the maturity of the software development process. These examples show how large organizations differ in the use of the SEI CMM. One organization is approaching level 4 and has been planning to collect process measurements. The other organization achieved level 3, but may not continue to level 4. Process measurements already have been collected over the years.

Case 1
Raytheon's Equipment Division, starting in 1988, used the SEI capability assessment questionnaire to benchmark the software process used in its software system laboratory (SSL). In five years, the SSL progressed (in sequence) from level 1 to level 3, as defined by the SEI CMM. As of 1995, the SSL aims at approaching level 4.

The SSL benefited from the increase in process maturity, which helped to reduce rework from "41% to 11%" of total project costs. In addition, progression to a higher maturity level helped to incur substantial return on investments.

Case 2
Corning Incorporated's Information Services Division used the SEI CMM to start assessment of its software process. A process improvement team was established to plan improvement activities. The SEI CMM proved to be useful "in planning and scheduling improvement efforts." The model helped the team to progress from level 1 to level 2, and then to level 3.

However, Corning made available to the team a set of metrics that was collected for a number of years, even before the company accepted the SEI CMM as the process improvement initiative. The company did not have to wait until it reached levels 4 and 5 to start measuring improvement processes. These metrics provided the rationale "to quantify achievements and to justify investments in the improvement initiative."

Quantitative evaluations of process performance should start in the early project stages. The importance of detecting software errors early in the development life cycle cannot be overlooked. Davis [18] suggests a hypothesis that "the later in the development life cycle that a software error is detected, the more expensive it will be to repair." According to study, the costs of repairing errors in the requirements phase of the development life cycle are much lower than the costs of detecting and repairing errors in the maintenance phase of the life cycle.

Cognitive bias

Theories and practices of risk management methodologies reflect the developer's thought processes. Stacy [19] discusses "how the biases might show up in day-to-day software engineering activities." For example, when developers test and debug software, their problem-solving techniques tend to be cognitive-biased.

Cognitive biases are more likely to occur when the developers' use their mental representations to handle random events. Examples of random events include probabilities and percentages as well as process improvement measurements of the risks. If properly used, cognitive bias on risk assessment and management could result in substantial savings on investments in software development processes.

Software developers use prior cognitive knowledge and experience to develop questionnaires. More flexible formal evaluation instruments to assess and manage risks should be developed in consideration of the cognitive bias of software development personnel. Cognitive issues have not been addressed in important software engineering models.

Notes

1. Existing users are referenced to check the ease of use, ease of change, and other risk factors of the component.

REFERENCES

[1] Humphrey, V. S., and W. L. Sweet, *A Method for Assessing the Software Engineering Capability of Contractors* (Technical Report CMU/SEI-87-TR-23, ESD/TR-87-186, Preliminary Version, Sept. 1987), Software Engineering Institute, Carnegie Mellon University, Pittsburgh, PA.

[2] Boehm, Barry W., "Section 2: Risk Management Priorities: The Six Basic Steps," *Software Risk Management,* Los Alamitos CA: IEEE Computer Society Press, 1989.

[3] Boehm, Barry W., "Section 1: Introduction and Overview," *Software Risk Management,* Alamitos CA: IEEE Computer Society Press, 1989.

[4] Boehm, Barry W., "A Spiral Model of Software Development and Enhancement," *Computer,* The Institute of Electrical and Electronics Engineers, May 1988.

[5] Vessy, Iris, and V. P. Sravanapudis, "CASE Tools: Collaborative Support Technologies," *Communications of the ACM,* Vol. 35, No. 1, Jan. 1995, pp. 83–94.

[6] McFarlan, F. Warren, "Portfolio approach to information systems," *The Harvard Business Review,* Jan./Feb. 1974.

[7] Williamson, Mickey, "Science of Software Development," *CIO,* April 15, 1996, pp. 62–68.

[8] Curtis, Bill, W. E. Hefley, S. Miller, and M. D. Konrad, *People Management Capability Maturity Model, Draft Version 0.2* (for public review), Software Engineering Institute, Pittsburgh, PA, Nov. 1994.

[9] Yourdan, Edward, *Rise and Resurrection of the American Programmer,* Upper Saddle River, NJ: Yourdan Press, 1996.

[10] Pualk, Mark C., M. D. Konrad, and S. M. Garcia, "CMM Versus SPICE Architecture," *Software Process Newsletter,* Vol. 13, No. 3, Software Engineering Technical Council, IEEE Computer Society, Spring 1995.

[11] Rae, Andrew, P. Robert, and H.-L. Hausen, *Software Evaluation for Certification: Principles, Practice and Legal Liability,* London, UK: McGraw-Hill Book Company, 1995.

[12] Vacca, John R., "Process Management Adapts Application Development to Users," *Application Development Trends,* Vol. 1, No. 1, March 11, 1994, pp. 51–55.

[13]   Garrett, Linda, "Product Review: LBMS' Process Engineer 2.5," *Application Development Trends*, Vol. 1, No. 12, Nov. 1994.

[14]   Yourdan, Edward, *Decline and Fall of American Programmers*, Englewood Cliffs, NJ: PTR Prentice-Hall, 1993.

[15]   Hasse, Volkmar, et al., "Bootstrap: Fine-Tuning Process Assessment, " *IEEE Software*, Vol. 11, No. 4, July 1994, pp. 25–45.

[16]   Bandinelli, Sergio, et al., "Modeling and Improving an Industrial Software Process," *IEEE Trans. on Software Engineering*, Vol. 21, No. 5, May 1995, pp. 440–454.

[17]   Johnson, D. L., and J. G. Brodman, "What small organizations say about the CMM, " *Proc. 16th Internal Conference Software Engineering* (ICSE 16), IEEE Computer Society, 1994.

[18]   Davis, Alan M., *Software Requirements: Objects, Functions, & States (Revision)*, Englewood Cliffs, NJ: PTR Prentice-Hall, 1993.

[19]   Stacy, Webb, and J. MacMillian, "Cognitive Bias in Software Engineering," *Communications of the ACM*, Vol. 38, No. 6, June 1995, pp. 57–65.

Part IV

Part IV is more detailed and contains six chapters on suggested applications of the risk management process to software engineering models. Each chapter focuses on each step of the risk management processes. They are, in respective order, asset valuations, security threats, security controls and tests, safeguards, economic value analysis, and reiterative processes.

Chapter 7

Asset valuations

A N *asset* IS defined as any resource needed to automate a system *for each stage of a software development life cycle*. Identifying and valuating the asset groups for each stage of software development life cycle (see Figure 7.1) is the first step in applying the risk management process to software engineering models.

This step overcomes the deficiencies of asset identification and valuations in software engineering models (see Chapter 3) and with software metrics (see Chapter 4). Two other deficiencies are noted. In the security arena (see Chapter 5), asset groups and their valuations are the same for each stage of the cycle. The assets, as described in software risk management theories (see Chapter 6), are narrower in scope (e.g., software is the only asset).

The asset categories are divided into basic and customized. Both asset categories may change from one stage to another in a life cycle Basic asset categories are tangible and serve as a template or a guideline. Management objectives can be broadened to include asset categories customized to suit a particular system, a system development project, and workflow processes (see

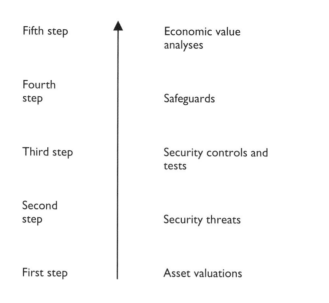

Fifth step — Economic value analyses

Fourth step — Safeguards

Third step — Security controls and tests

Second step — Security threats

First step — Asset valuations

Figure 7.1 Asset valuation is the first step in risk management processes.

Figure 7.2). Customized asset categories consists of both tangible and intangible items. For example, magnetic tapes are a tangible asset. A compliance plan on the use and disposition of the tapes is an intangible asset.

The ratio of tangible asset items and intangible asset items may differ in each stage. The general rule is the more complex a software development project is, the more likely that the asset categories and the ratio between tangible and intangible assets will change from one stage to another.

Without asset categories, the assets cannot be valuated. The asset valuations are needed to determine replacement costs, if any, of the assets. Once the replacement costs have been calculated, they must be justified. Costs of tangible assets are quantifiable (e.g., depreciated costs, cost estimates, and actual dollars).

Relative values are used to determine the importance of intangible assets. To quantify the costs of intangible assets, a table of criteria should be developed to cross-reference the relative values with the replacement costs of the assets. Management objectives determine what relative values should be assigned to what replacement costs.

The resultant valuations of tangible and intangible assets, along with the savings of implementing safeguards, are used as inputs to economic feasibility studies. These studies will recommend actions that aim at eliminating or mitigating high risks to the assets to more acceptable levels.

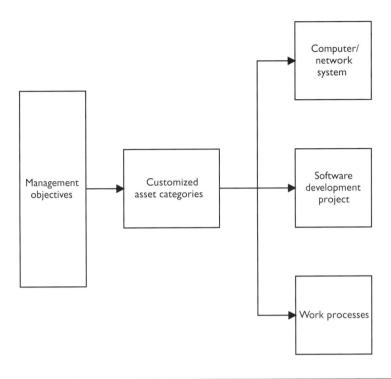

Figure 7.2 Management objectives receive feedback on customization of asset categories.

This chapter gives examples of asset categories and valuations. Subsequent chapters discuss assets and their valuations as inputs in later stages of applying risk management processes to the models. In particular, they look at how risks become threats to asset groups, how security controls and tests are used to identify lack or deficiencies of safeguards for specific assets, how to determine safeguards to protect the assets, and how economic value analyses are used to calculate asset loss probabilities.

7.1 Basic asset categories

For a computer system, assets are arbitrarily divided into the following categories within an ADP system of activity:

- Hardware;
- Software;

- Physical;
- Personnel;
- Administrative;
- Data;
- Communications.

Each category is further divided into subgroups, with examples in Sections 7.1.1 through 7.1.7. These subgroups may change from one stage to another in the life cycle.

7.1.1 Hardware assets

Hardware is grouped into central machines, storage medium, special interface equipment, and input/output (I/O) devices. Types and use of hardware may change from one stage of the cycle to another. A *central machine* is further broken down into central processing unit (CPU), main memory, I/O channels, and an operator's console. Other attributes can be added to the central machine category, depending on the complexity of the system.

Storage medium consists of optical, paper, and magnetic media. Optical disks are available in both read only and writable formats. Paper media covers punched cards, paper tape, and paper printout. Magnetic media include the following:

- Disk packs;
- Portable/removable hard disks;
- Nonremovable hard disks;
- Credit card disks;
- Magnetic tapes;
- Flopticals;
- Diskettes (floppies);
- Cassettes.

Special interface equipment includes network front ends, database machines, and intelligent controllers. Middleware servers should be classified as special interface technologies.

I/O devices are grouped into user-directed and storage. The following is a partial list of user-directed I/O devices:

- Printers;
- Plotters;
- Image capture devices;
- Keyboards;
- Mice;
- Other "pointing" input devices;
- Terminals;
- Video displays.

Among the storage I/O devices are external and internal disks, tapes, and CD-ROM drives for standard desktop computers. Other examples include PCMCIA cards that can be used on both the notebooks and desktop computers.

7.1.2 **Software assets**

Software assets cover operating systems and systems and applications software. Due to the portability of most software packages, it is more likely that some software assets will change from one cycle stage to another.

Operating systems are software programs that control computer resources. The type of resources provided depends on the operating systems. In turn, the type of operating system depends on the hardware on which it is used.

Resources include scheduling, debugging, in-output control, compilation, storage assignment, data management, linkage, security, and related services. They control how software, such as standards applications, systems utilities, test programs, and communications, are compiled, run, debugged, and assigned queue priorities and access controls.

7.1.3 **Physical assets**

The physical asset category is concerned with environmental systems, buildings, computer facilities, backup facilities, and supplies. It is obvious that supplies are most likely, and computer and backup facilities least likely, to change from one life cycle to another. The following are items associated with *environmental systems*:

- Air conditioning;
- Power;
- Water;

- Lighting;
- Pollution.

The *building* subcategory is concerned with buildings that house personnel, software, hardware, administrative, data, and communications assets. They include buildings on site and at remote sites.

Computer facilities include the following:

- Computer rooms;
- Tape libraries;
- Magnetic disk libraries;
- Optical disk libraries;
- Computer engineer rooms;
- Physical plant rooms.

The *backup facility* subcategory is concerned with auxiliary power, auxiliary environmental controls, and auxiliary supplies to maintain, for example, libraries of backup tapes and disks. Magnetic media, paper, and ribbons are good examples of the *supplies* subcategory.

7.1.4 Personnel assets

Personnel assets include computer personnel, building personnel, and installation management personnel. *Computer personnel* may change from one cycle stage to another, depending on the complexity of a development project, and may consist of, for example, the following:

- Supervisory personnel;
- Systems analysts;
- Software engineers;
- Information systems personnel;
- Applications programmers;
- Systems programmers;
- Operators;
- Librarians;
- Security officers;
- Risk managers;

- Maintenance personnel;
- Temporary employee and consultants;
- System evaluators and auditors;
- Clerical personnel;
- Help desk personnel.

7.1.5 Administrative assets

The administrative asset category consists of documentation, operations, procedures, inventory records, and operational procedures. They differ from one cycle stage to another. The following is a list of *documentation* samples:

- Software;
- Application;
- Hardware;
- File;
- Program;
- Job control language (JCL);
- Information system;
- Hypertext help.

Operations is concerned with schedules, operating guidelines, and manuals, as well as audit documents. *Procedures* includes emergency plans, contingency plans, risk analysis and management, security procedures, I/O procedures, and integrity controls. *Inventory records* are important in keeping records of software, hardware, and documentation. Vital record, priority-run schedules, and production procedures come under *operational procedures*.

7.1.6 Data assets

Data may consist of one more of the following types: classified, operations, tactical, financial, statistical, personnel, and logistics. Each data type may overlap another.

Classified data is concerned with the level of data classification, ranging from unclassified to secret. *Operations* data pertains to payroll, personnel, and other categories that require daily operations. *Tactical* data pertains to data on military maneuvers and operations. *Logistics* data concerns military procurement, maintenance, and movement of equipment, supplies, and personnel.

7.1.7 Communications assets

Communications equipment assets include communications lines, communications processors, multiplexors, switching devices, telephones, and cables. Also included are cellular and landline modems and wireless input devices.

7.2 Customized asset categories

This section discusses briefly how an asset category template can be customized for a software development project. Customized asset categories include tangible and intangible assets. For illustrative purposes, the following examples give tangible, intangible, and mixed assets.

7.2.1 Tangible asset items

Tangible asset items are easier to identify than intangible asset items. The number of asset categories to be declared depends on management objectives, system type, project complexity, and the range of work processes.

Let's assume a management objective can declare the following seven asset groups for a software development project:

- Hardware;
- Software;
- Facility;
- Human resources;
- Office administration;
- Data warehouse;
- Communication.

Group items can be added or removed (see Figure 7.3) if the changes in management objectives on assets to be protected in the systems, projects, and workflow processes are significant. In the following example, documentation files and data classification are two items declared as assets:

- Computers;
- Software;
- Documentation files;
- Human resources;

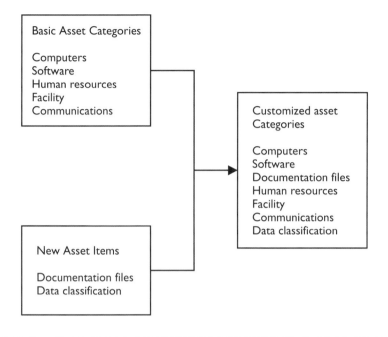

Figure 7.3 Customized asset categories for a computer system.

- Facility;
- Communications;
- Data classification.

The customized template can be revised for another project that uses a network to develop software (see Figure 7.4). In the following, a network asset group has been added:

- Hardware;
- Software;
- Physical;
- Human resources;
- Office administration;
- Data and files;
- Network.

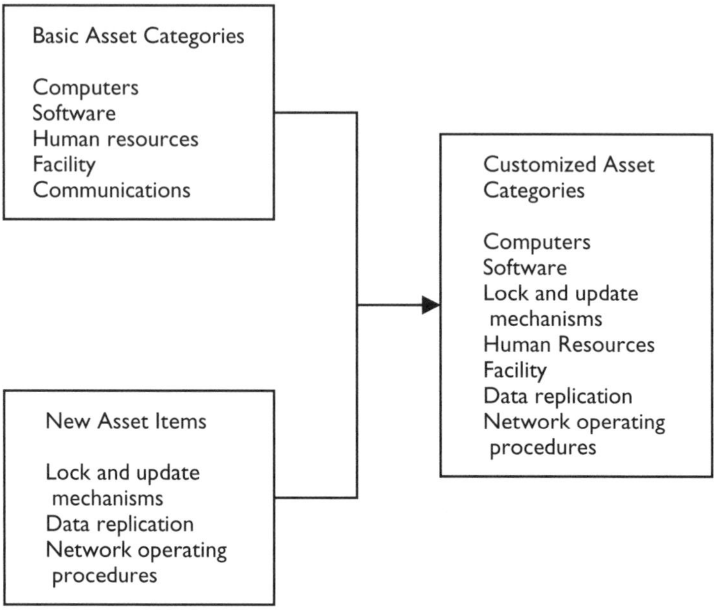

Figure 7.4   Customized asset categories for a network system.

In another scenario, the following shows that data replication, lock and update mechanisms, as well as network operating procedures have been declared as assets:

- Computers;
- Software;
- Lock and update mechanisms;
- Human resources;
- Facility;
- Data replication;
- Network operating procedures.

7.2.2 Intangible asset items

All software development consists of both tangible and intangible assets (see Figure 7.5). Grouping of intangible assets is arbitrary. These assets, for example, can be broken into plan, organization, technical, and external factors.

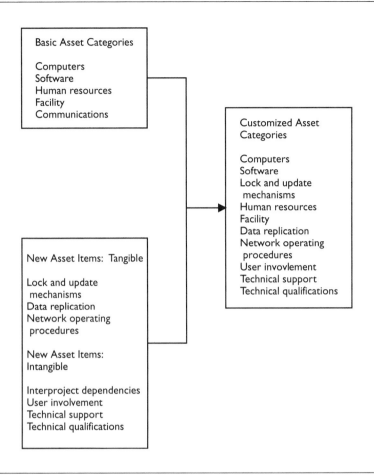

Figure 7.5 Tangible and intangible assets.

Intangible assets have the potential to influence the successful completion of each stage. The uncertainty of each asset varies from one development stage to another, and has a potential impact on the success of the project. New intangible assets may be introduced unexpectedly in any stage of the development.

Intangible assets in the external factor category include vendor support, interproject dependencies, and IS plan compliance. The assets in the organizational category include user involvement and size of departments. The technical category focuses on the assets that provide technical support, technical qualifications, and training.

7.3 Asset valuations

The abbreviated risk method (see Chapter 5) is used to manage risks to the assets of computers connected to networks, minicomputers, and other server types of medium scale. This can be applied to the software engineering models and provides good examples of how the assets are grouped and valuated for each stage of software development cycle—from initial to operations.

The valuations should include factors that can raise or lower the original costs of the assets. They can be represented by a probability factor over a period of time, such as one year or three years, depending on management objectives.

For example, the costs of replacing the personnel will increase. Annual increases in salaries and promotions, and additions of software development personnel, are obviously contributing factors. This is true if the turnover of personnel is low.

In another example, some hardware costs could depreciate over a period of time. If damaged, the hardware could be replaced with the same model at less cost (it also could cost more with a newer model).

It would be advantageous to use a software package that keeps track of software and hardware assets. It should be helpful in maintaining inventories of the assets that could change from one stage to another in a software development life cycle.

Tables 7.1 through 7.4 give brief examples of valuation data sheets. Each data sheet discusses briefly threat impacts and replacement cost justifications.

Table 7.1 An Example of a Data Sheet on Hardware Assets for Each Stage of the Development Life Cycle

Valuation Data Sheet: Hardware Assets	
System	Atlantic Warehouse Tracking Client/Server System
Location	Anywhere, USA
Total Assets	
Development stage 1	$100,000*
Development stage 2	$110,000*
Development stage 3	$100,000*

Table 7.1 (continued)

Valuation Data Sheet: Hardware Assets	
Development stage 4	$100,000*
Development stage 5	$150,000*

Threat Impacts

The hardware assets can be damaged or destroyed if adequate measures of safeguarding them are not taken, particularly for the servers. One or two client workstations could be used as backup workstations.

Replacement Costs Justifications

The costs are based on replacement costs for newer models. Technology evolves faster than the safeguards to counter the risks.

---

* The detailed costs for each hardware component is attached to this data sheet. Quantity, device type, model number, serial number or other identifying number, as well as probability factors of cost changes are included.

Table 7.2 An Example of a Data Sheet on Software Assets for Each Stage of the Development Life Cycle

Valuation Data Sheet: Software Assets	
System	Atlantic Warehouse Tracking Client/Server System
Location	Anywhere, USA
Total Assets	
Development stage 1	$100*
Development stage 2	$100*
Development stage 3	$100*
Development stage 4	$100*
Development stage 5	$100*

Table 7.2 (continued)

Threat Impacts

The software assets can be damaged or destroyed if measures of safeguarding them are inadequate. Backup tapes and disks (as permitted by software license agreements) are available as safeguards to counter the risks to software assets.

Replacement Costs Justifications

The costs for software assets were based on the estimated time needed to restore software from backup tapes and disks stored at an off-site location. The time was estimated to be two hours times hourly wage rates of two members of the system administration staff. The hourly rates will change annually effective the first week of January.

---

* A detailed list of software packages are attached to this data sheet. Quantity, software name, vendor name, and serial number or other identifying number are included.

Table 7.3   An Example of a Data Sheet on Personnel Assets for Each Stage of the Development Life Cycle

Valuation Data Sheet: Personnel Assets

System	Atlantic Warehouse Tracking Client/Server System
Location	Anywhere, USA
Total Assets	
Development stage 1	$25,000*
Development stage 2	$25,000*
Development stage 3	$25,000*
Development stage 4	$25,000*
Development stage 5	$25,000*

Threat Impacts

The system administrator may (least likely) perish in an airplane or car crash while a stage of development cycle is in progress.

Replacement Costs Justifications

Costs for personnel assets were based on the estimated time needed to retrain personnel to perform existing system administrator functions. The time was estimated to be six months of training for one system administrator. Salaries will increase annually as of the first week of January.

---

* This data sheet may need to be revised later to reflect changes in training costs.

Table 7.4   An Example of a Data Sheet on Documentation Assets for Each Stage of the Development Life Cycle

Valuation Data Sheet: Documentation Assets	
System	Atlantic Warehouse Tracking Client/Server System
Location	Anywhere, USA
Total Assets	
Development Stage 1	$0*
Development Stage 2	$0*
Development Stage 3	$0*
Development Stage 4	$0*
Development Stage 5	$0*

Threat Impacts

The manuals can be damaged or destroyed if measures of safeguarding them are inadequate. Manual copies (as permitted by software license agreements) are available as safeguards to counter the risks to software assets.

Replacement Costs Justifications

No cost was associated due to the availability of manual copies for popular software packages.

* A detailed list of manuals for popular software packages is attached to this data sheet. Quantity, manual title, vendor name, and other identifying items are included. None of the software are proprietary.

Chapter 8

Security threats

A THREAT, IN CHAPTER 5 on security, is defined as any possible harm to the system. It results in significant damage to or loss of (at least) a resource required by the system. A vulnerability, according to Russell [1], is a weakness in a computer system or a point where the system is susceptible to attack. A risk is the probability that a particular security threat will exploit a particular system vulnerability, according to Russell.

In this chapter, threat, vulnerability, and risk are redefined (see Figure 8.1). The definition for threat can be expanded to include any possible harm to an asset, tangible or intangible, in *any stage of a software engineering model that focuses on the development life cycle*. Likewise, the definition for vulnerability can be reworded to include weaknesses in a project that is susceptible to a threat attack in any stage of the model. Similarly, the definition for risk can be expanded to include a security threat that will exploit a project vulnerability in any stage of the model. The list of threats and vulnerabilities and probabilities of risks need not be the same for each stage of the development life cycle.

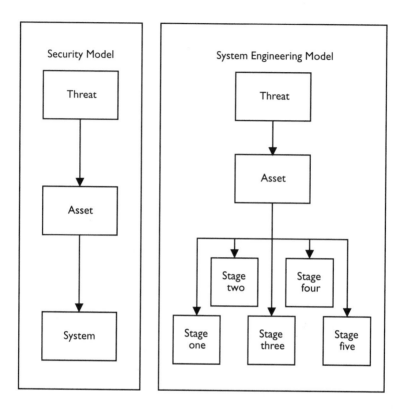

Figure 8.1 Threats to the security of a system are redefined to include threats to an asset for any stage of a development life cycle.

Security threats to the assets must be identified after the assets are identified and valuated. Some threats are significant; others are insignificant or inapplicable. Identifying security threat categories for each stage of a software development life cycle (see Figure 8.2) is the second step in applying risk management processes to software engineering models. Threat categories considered significant provide inputs to security controls and tests (see Chapter 9).

This step overcomes the deficiencies of threat identifications in software engineering models (see Chapter 3) and with software metrics (see Chapter 4). Two other deficiencies are noted. In the security arena (see Chapter 5), threats so identified are the same for each stage of the cycle. The threats, as described in software risk management theories (see Chapter 6), are narrower in scope.

To identify threat categories, one should keep in mind two things: the vulnerabilities and the impact of threats on each asset category, as discussed in Chapter 9. The vulnerabilities are used to identify the weaknesses of each stage

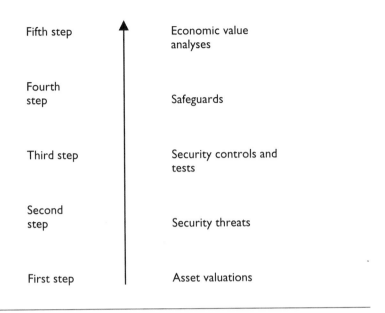

Fifth step	Economic value analyses
Fourth step	Safeguards
Third step	Security controls and tests
Second step	Security threats
First step	Asset valuations

Figure 8.2   Security threat categories is the second step in risk management processes.

of the development life cycle (e.g., the model). Impacts of threats on each asset category range from not applicable to very high. If the impact on an asset does not apply, it should not be considered in the risk management processes.

Threats, vulnerabilities, and probabilities of risk can change, in varying degree, from one stage to another. Threats may exist in one stage and not in another stage. Vulnerabilities in the system susceptible to a threat attack may exist for one stage and not in another stage for the same threat attack. Likewise, probabilities of risks can change from one stage to another to the degree a particular security threat can exploit a particular system vulnerability. For a complex project, the degree of compound risks may change from one stage to another.

The threats, vulnerabilities, and risk probabilities may be used as standard templates. Similar to customized assets, the templates can be tailored to suit a particular project or a specific stage of the life development cycle. The templates are repeatable processes and should be automated on a client/server system.

If the templates are automated, they should be flexible enough to allow changes for technology that evolves quicker than the safeguards to counter the vulnerabilities and risks. For example, when laptops or notebooks became popular, the threat of notebook mobility was added to the template of threats. This template is normally applicable to the assets of desktop and floor computers used to develop software products.

The vulnerabilities of inadequate measures to protect the laptops from theft due to mobility are greater than the vulnerabilities of inadequate measures to protect the desktop and floor computers from theft. Obviously, the laptops are much smaller in size, weigh much less, and are much easier to carry around than the desktop computers.

A laptop has been reported left, by an unauthorized user, in airport waiting rooms and not found in a lost and found department. Those that were unintentionally left behind did not have boot-up, supervisory protection modes, or hard disk passwords and antitheft devices. Anyone who found the laptop had unauthorized access to the data.

To ensure the templates are periodically updated, management objectives should be established or reviewed, as technology significantly changes. The objectives should consider the identification of threats an important part of a risk management program. Without threat identification, it is not possible to determine what vulnerabilities are, how much protection is required, and how much protection exists.

This chapter gives examples of security threat categories and sample data sheets.

8.1 Security threat categories

The concepts of the checklist risk method and abbreviated risk method, as discussed in Chapter 5, can be applied to security threats in any one stage of development life cycle. The threats in the checklist method are easier to group than those for the abbreviated method. The abbreviated risk method considers the impact of a threat for all assets identified for each life cycle stage. The impact of a threat on an asset varies from inapplicable to very high.

8.1.1 Checklist risk method

This section gives examples of threats under various categories. Assume a management objective declares seven threat categories for one stage of a software development life cycle. The threat categories are named hardware, software, human resources, facility, data mechanisms, disaster recovery procedures, and organizational resources.

The first seven are tangible threat categories and the last threat category is an intangible threat category. Intangible threat categories have not yet been addressed in computer the security arena.

The following are suggested items for each threat category.

- *Hardware threat,* including theft, fire, water damage, high temperature, high humidity, unshielded network cables, inadequate maintenance contract, inadequate power switch lock, and unauthorized hardware alteration. Also included are hardware failure, encryption devices not installed, inadequate protection against signals emanating from computers and networks, inadequate antitheft devices for laptops, power instability and outages, and equipment not provided with an uninterruptable power supply.

- *Software threat,* including malicious viruses, unauthorized disclosure of passwords, system crash, outdated user manuals, copyright violations, inadequate software inventory, inadequate software library controls, lack of configuration controls, and unsecured original software.

- *Human resource threat,* including disgruntled employees; industrial spies; inadequate training; high turnover; hostile user, careless user, unintentional programmer, and operator errors; inadequate background check of the users; insufficient funds for security training; and inadequate employee incentive programs.

- *Facility threat,* including poorly secured building and computer areas; defective electronic alarms and monitoring devices; inadequate heating, cooling, and humidity control systems; inadequate inspections of water/steam pipes located near hardware units; malfunctioning fire and smoke alarms; lack of emergency lighting; and inadequate protection from static electricity. Also included are smoking and food/drinks permitted near the computers, improper fire extinguishers, inadequate visitor controls, inadequate cleaning schedule, lack of water detectors, emergency phone numbers not posted in appropriate areas, combustible materials in computer areas, and unmarked emergency exits.

- *Data mechanisms threat,* including screen display of inadequate warning message against unauthorized access, sensitive hardcopy output unattended, inadequate data encryption, inadequate user privileges, inadequate password controls, system unattended, residual data attached to a file,[1] unlimited logon attempts, sensitive data files not identified and protected, excessive file fragmentation, unauthorized disclosure of data, magnetic media not cleaned and tested at regular intervals, defective write mechanisms on disks, and removable media not properly labeled and secured.

- *Disaster recovery procedures threat,* including inadequate procedures to expand suddenly processing capability to accommodate an emergency at another site, unavailability of loaner equipment, poorly written disaster recovery procedures, inadequate backup copies of sensitive files and original programs not stored off site, outdated procedures to take action when the system is impaired, inadequate recovery plan testing procedures, inadequate network operating procedures, and lack of agreement for backup operations with another facility.

- *Organizational resources threat,* including inadequate user involvement, unavailability of key users, poor vendor support, extensive recruitment, inadequate user areas, overdependence on suppliers, poor technical support, and inappropriate technical qualifications.

8.1.2 Abbreviated risk method

This section gives examples of a broader range of threats for an abbreviated risk method for a stage of the development life cycle. Management objectives may declare some items listed under a threat category for the checklist risk method as threat categories for the abbreviated risk method. As shown in Figure 8.3, unintentional programmer error is an item under the human resource threat category. Management objectives declare this item as a threat category.

Each data sheet, as discussed in Chapter 9, begins with a threat category. The category must be short and clearly stated. If the category is ambiguous, it must be clarified.

For example, fire is a threat category. This category may be ambiguous in a large organization. It does not say where in the organization the threat of fire may occur—in the central computer room or a remote site housing several minicomputers as primary servers. The location of a fire threat category must be clearly stated (see Figure 8.4).

As another example, water damage is a threat category. It does not indicate where in a large organization the threat of water damage may occur—in a large LAN server room at the headquarters or at numerous remote areas for 25,000 users across the nation. The location of water damage threat category must be clearly stated.

Russell and others suggest three groups of threats: natural, unintentional, and intentional. Natural threats are clearly distinct from unintentional and intentional threats. A threat may be distinctly unintentional, but not intentional. Another threat may be either unintentional or intentional. They apply to both distributed and nondistributed computer systems.

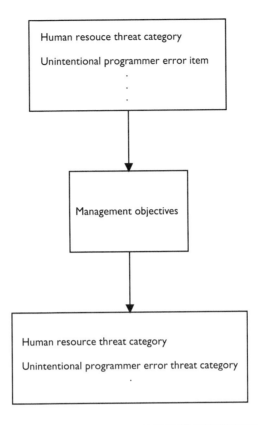

Figure 8.3 Management objectives treat unintentional programmer error, an item under the human resources threat category, as a threat category.

Of particular importance in a distributed computer system are communication threats that are obviously intentional. Russell and others suggest four types of communications threats: (1) a masquerade, (2) a playback or a replay, (3) repudiation, and (4) denial service. They each play a role, to more or less extent, in industrial espionage. An example of each threat is given below:

- *Masquerade:* Another user pretends to be authorized user.
- *Playback or replay:* A user records a legitimate record or message and resends it without proper authorization.
- *Repudiation:* A user denies sending or receiving a message (no receipt of return).

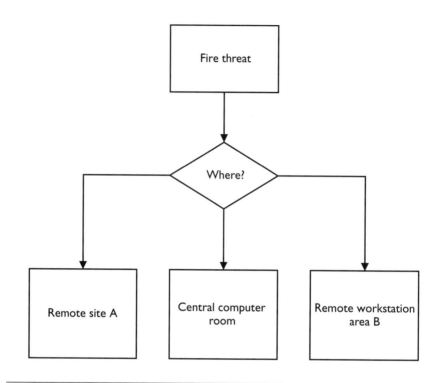

Figure 8.4   Location of a fire threat category must be determined.

- *Denial of service:* A user floods the system with files, records, or messages, thus dominating, stopping, or degrading the system.

Natural and physical threats cannot always be prevented. However, management can minimize the chance of damage to computer equipment with, for example, a sprinkler system, a smoking and eating policy, and a disaster plan to arrange for a backup system at another site. These threats are divided into natural, environmental, and internal. Natural and physical threats are easier to group than intentional and unintentional threats.

The following is a list of sample threat categories for the first stage of a development life cycle. Specific locations and types of these categories are not provided due to lack of space in this chapter. Threat categories in later stages of a life cycle may not be applicable to the first stage.

- *Natural threats:*
  Floods;
  Earthquakes;

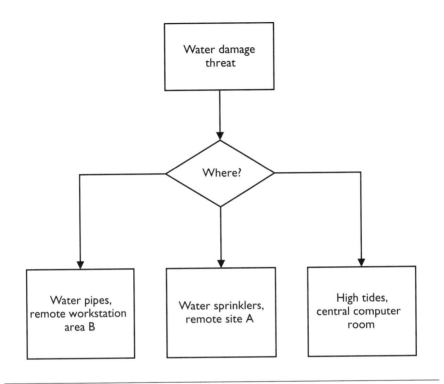

Figure 8.5   Location of a water damage threat category must be determined.

Mud slides;
Hurricanes.

- *External threats:*

Aircraft crashes;
Power failures;
Water sprinkling system failures.

- *Internal threats:*

Smoking;
Soda and coffee spills;
Dust accumulation.

Intentional threats occur when the attackers and industrial spies have computing resources, time, and money to, for example, "intercept and decipher electromagnetic emanations, or perform a determined cryptographic analysis" [1]. These threats are of two types: insiders and outsiders. The grouping of the following threats into insiders and outsiders is left to the reader:

- Unauthorized system access;
- Unauthorized software alteration;
- System crash;
- Unauthorized file/database alteration;
- Foreign intelligence agents;
- Terrorists, raiders, and crackers;
- Unauthorized disclosure;
- Unauthorized users with basic programming skills;
- Unauthorized use of assembly language utilities;
- Unauthorized booting from a floppy drive;
- Communications threats;
- Unauthorized encryption device alteration;
- Unauthorized hardware alteration;
- Unauthorized physical access;
- Theft;
- Sabotage and vandalism.

Unintentional threats refer to threats of user and system administrator ignorance. For example, a user may accidentally wipe out a large, primary mainframe database when using a database management system package to upgrade the software on a client workstation. These threats could be divided into at least three groups: inadequate training, inadequate procedures, and ignorance. Each group may overlap one another.

The following are examples of unintentional threats:

- *Inadequate procedures:*

  Inadequate software library controls;
  Inadequate lock and update mechanisms;
  Inadequate software configuration controls;
  Lack of disk management controls;
  Inadequate employee incentive programs;
  Unsecured facility;
  Inadequate visitor controls.

- *Inadequate training:*

    Unintentional software developer error;
    Unintentional programmer error;
    Unintentional user error;
    Inadequate security training;
    Inadequate heating, cooling, and humidity control systems;
    Inadequate disaster/recovery plan;
    Inadequate personnel staffing;
    Inadequate user involvement.

- *Ignorance:*

    Power failure/fluctuation;
    Inadequate data classification controls;
    Inadequate administrative controls;
    Inadequate security inspection controls;
    Unprotected password file;
    Inadvertent file deletion;
    Inadequate disk disabling controls.

Unintentional/intentional threats are threats that could be intentional under certain conditions or unintentional under other conditions. The following are examples of unintentional/intentional threats:

- Hardware failure;
- Software failure;
- Fire;
- Water damage;
- Disgruntled employees;
- Computer-literate moles;
- Industrial spies.

8.2 Sample data sheets

Tables 8.1–8.9 are sample data sheets, each showing the threat category component. Other aspects of the data sheets will be discussed in Chapter 9.

Table 8.1   Sample Data Sheet on Natural Threat Category on Floods (External)

Threat Data Sheet	
Category	Natural threat
Subcategory	External
Type	Floods
Scope	Facility about one mile from Orleans River, which rises with high tides
Average frequency	Twice a year
Historical damage	None

Table 8.2   Sample Data Sheet on Physical Threat Category on Soda and Coffee Spills (Internal)

Threat Data Sheet	
Category	Physical threat
Subcategory	Internal
Type	Soda and coffee spills
Scope	Sodas and coffee cups next to desktop computer drives, and keyboard
Average frequency	Ten times a year
Historical damage	Sodas and coffee spilled on unprotected keyboards

Table 8.3   Sample Data Sheet on Intentional Threat Category on Unauthorized System Access (Insiders)

Threat Data Sheet	
Category	Intentional threat
Subcategory	Insiders
Type	Unauthorized system access

Threat Data Sheet	
Scope	Employees with programming skills who can change file attributes and decipher system files
Average frequency	One incident since a year ago
Historical damage	Operating system crashed, corrupting the directories and files

Table 8.4 Sample Data Sheet on Intentional Threat Category on Communication Threats (Outsiders)

Threat Data Sheet	
Category	Intentional threat
Subcategory	Outsiders
Type	Communications threats
Scope	Masquerade and denial of service
Average frequency	Four times a year
Historical damage	An outsider pretended to be an authorized user. About three or four authorized users flooded the system with files, records, or messages thus dominating, stopping, or degrading the system

Table 8.5 Sample Data Sheet on Unintentional Threat Category on Lack of Disk Management Controls (Inadequate Procedures)

Threat Data Sheet	
Category	Unintentional threat
Subcategory	Inadequate procedures
Type	Lack of disk management controls
Scope	Hard disks (removable and nonremovable) and PCMCIA hard cards)
Average frequency	Three times a year
Historical damage	High fragmentation of files on a hard disk (magnetic or PCMCIA) resulting in disk crashes

Table 8.6 Sample Data Sheet on Unintentional Threat Category on Unintentional Software Developer Error (Inadequate Training)

Threat Data Sheet

Category	Unintentional threat
Subcategory	Inadequate training
Type	Unintentional software developer error
Scope	Software developer for financial system projects
Average frequency	200 times a year
Historical damage	Numerous development errors caught at the end of project cycle resulted in project rework cost overruns and late delivery of the system due to lack of training on software development

Table 8.7 Sample Data Sheet on Unintentional Threat Category on Power Failure/Fluctuation (Ignorance)

Threat Data Sheet

Category	Unintentional threat
Subcategory	Ignorance
Type	Power failure/fluctuation
Scope	Power source for file servers in main computer room
Average frequency	Twice a year
Historical damage	Power failure or fluctuations caused brownouts of the servers

Table 8.8 Sample Data Sheet on Unintentional Threat Category, Such As Inadvertent File Deletion (Ignorance)

Threat Data Sheet	
Category	Unintentional threat
Subcategory	Ignorance
Type	Inadvertent file deletion
Scope	Users/programmers make simple upgrade to software
Average frequency	Three times a year
Historical damage	Important files were inadvertently deleted. File backups were not available

Table 8.9 Sample Data Sheet on Intentional/Unintentional Threat Category, Such As Disgruntled Employees

Threat Data Sheet	
Category	Unintentional/intentional threat
Subcategory	NA
Type	Disgruntled employees
Scope	Employees who received a notice of layoffs or demotions or who have unsatisfactory relationships with their supervisors
Average frequency	Once since a year ago
Historical damage	A disgruntled employee accidentally deleted all .ini files. However this same employee intentionally changed the internal commands in an operating system

Notes

1.　Residual data are created when a user modifies an original file to make it shorter. The shorter file attaches itself to the residual data from the previous file. This residual data is hidden when the shorter file appears, for example, on a document screen in a word processing program on a personal computer. To see the contents of the residual data, the user must use a disk management utility program, such as that provided by Norton Utilities. Since the residual data may contain sensitive information, it must be removed periodically with a utility program.

Reference

[1]　Russell, Deborah, and G. T. Gengemi, Sr., *Computer Security Books,* Sebastopol, CA: O'Reilly & Associates., 1991.

Chapter 9

Security controls and tests

SECURITY CONTROLS are concerned with mechanisms, already in place, for establishing a secure computer or network system. Security tests of the controls take place after security threats are identified. They determine what vulnerabilities can be identified to pinpoint weaknesses of the system that are susceptible to an attack or a threat (tangible or intangible).

If vulnerabilities exist, the results of the tests should list what additional security controls are required to reduce the risks to more acceptable levels. Additional controls will incur economic savings from having recovered from the damaged, destroyed, or lost assets. The probability of the costs of implementing additional controls to replace the assets will be less than the probability of the costs of *not* implementing the additional controls. In very rare cases, additional controls may be not required, because management has already implemented a security policy.

Depending on the risks to which a system is vulnerable, some security controls and tests are significant; others are insignificant or inapplicable. The more complex the system becomes, the more likely the risks to the system will be complex and compounded. The less complex the system is, the more likely the risks can be divided into standard categories.

Security controls may exist in one stage and not in another stage. Assuming a security control remains the same for each stage, vulnerabilities may exist in one stage and not in another.

If security controls change in response to evolving technologies, changing management objectives and expanding security policies, tests should be conducted to determine what security controls, previously insignificant, are now significant. The tests should also determine what security controls, previously declared significant, are now insignificant, and what security controls, unique to the system, should be added. Most important of all, the changes in security controls should result in greater economic savings in protecting the assets from the threats.

Security controls that are applicable to most systems may be used as standard templates. As with customized assets and security threats, the templates can be tailored to suit a particular situation of a particular project or a specific stage of the life development cycle. The templates are repeatable processes and should be automated on a client/server system. They should be flexible enough to allow changes, for technology evolves quicker than the safeguards to counter the vulnerabilities.

To ensure the templates are periodically updated, management objectives should be established or reviewed as technology significantly changes. The objectives should consider the identification of threats an important part of a risk management program. Without threat identification, it is not possible to determine what vulnerabilities exist.

Examples of templates include a list of questions for a particular security control for the checklist risk method. Also included is a standard list of vulnerabilities grouped under a security control for the abbreviated risk method.

Identifying security controls and tests for each stage of a software development life cycle (see Figure 9.1) is the third step in applying risk management processes to software engineering models. Threat categories considered significant provide inputs to security controls and tests.

This step overcomes the deficiencies of security control and vulnerability identification in software engineering models (see Chapter 3) and with software metrics (see Chapter 4). Two other deficiencies are noted. In the security arena (see Chapter 5), identified vulnerabilities are the same for each stage of the cycle. Specific vulnerabilities are not covered in the software risk management theories discussed in Chapter 6. Security controls may be covered under the category of risk management techniques, but are narrower in scope. Risk management techniques are treated the same for each stage of a life cycle project.

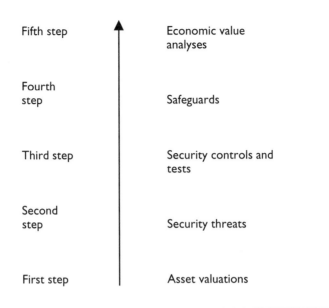

Figure 9.1   Security controls and tests is the third step in risk management processes.

To identify what security controls are already in place and are required, one should keep in mind that controls differ among personal computer workstations, network systems, minicomputers, and mainframes. The differences in controls are attributed, in part, to the unique characteristics and vulnerabilities of the operating systems and hardware configurations.

As discussed in Chapter 8, the definition for vulnerability includes weaknesses in a project that is susceptible to a threat attack in any stage of a software engineering model that focuses on the development life cycle (see Figure 9.2). Likewise, security controls can be extended to controls in any stage of the model. A list of security controls and tests need not be the same for each stage of the development life cycle.

This chapter gives vulnerability examples, security control and test categories, and sample data sheets on vulnerabilities.

9.1 **Vulnerability examples**

The following give examples of vulnerabilities in personal computer and network environments. These vulnerabilities require security controls, to be discussed later in this chapter.

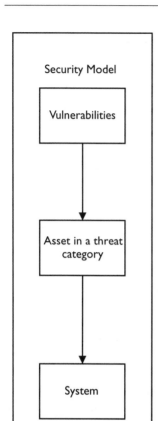
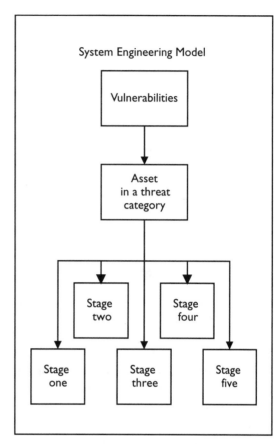

Figure 9.2 Vulnerabilities in a system are redefined to include vulnerabilities for any stage of a development life cycle.

No two networks are identical in nature or scope. Regardless of the simplicity or complexity of the network, a network environment introduces the need to focus attention on physical security. The chances of fire, water, natural disaster, and industrial espionage increase as a network extends across organizational sites. With the increased population of users accessing information assets on the network, the greater the chances for unauthorized use are.

Any computer network automatically introduces the risk of unauthorized access to a system. The hackers have used dialup telephones and network technologies to gain illegal system access. The hackers exploit the weaknesses in software access controls to enter the system itself.

Many software developers (particularly those on the Internet) leave their machines up and running and accessible by the networks 24 hours a day, seven days a week. They give hackers many more opportunities to break into a system (or an entire suite of systems).

9.2 Security control and test categories

The concepts of the checklist risk method and the abbreviated risk method, as discussed in Chapter 5, can be applied to security controls and tests in any one stage of a development life cycle. The controls and tests in the checklist are easier to group than those for the abbreviated method. The abbreviated risk method considers a security control for all assets identified for each stage of life cycle. The security control for an asset varies from inapplicable to very high.

9.2.1 Checklist risk method

This section gives examples of security controls and tests under various categories. The categories in the security arena may differ from those categories for systems engineering models. Management objectives determine which of the following three options should be used in developing categories:

- Security controls categories should be in parallel with threat categories.
- Security controls categories should be established that bear little resemblance to threat categories.
- Security categories should be established that reflect a mix of the two options.

However, for illustrative purposes, the categories for security controls and threats are in parallel.

In the previous chapter, management objectives have declared eight threat categories for one stage of software development life cycle. The threat categories are named as hardware, software, human resources, facility, data mechanisms, disaster recovery procedures, and organizational resources. The first seven are tangible threat categories and the last threat category is an intangible threat category.

In this section, the categories for threats and security controls are the same, although the items differ for each category. One security control category has been added to reflect the main feature of a distributed computer system. This category is called communications security controls.

The following are suggested items for each security controls category:

- *Hardware security controls,* including protection against hardware alteration, protection against hardware failure and hardware components, barcoding or other means of identifying equipment, making sure the system is not left on and unattended, periodic maintenance of hardware, allowing only authorized personnel to work on hardware, training of system personnel on emergency shutdown procedures, periodic maintenance of hardware inventory, and control of access to hardware.

- *Software security controls,* including compliance with copyright laws and license agreements/contracts, prohibition of the use of unapproved software, protection against theft and unauthorized reproduction, inspection of new software for infection, maintenance of backup copies, maintenance of software inventory, availability of software/applications documentation, establishment of configuration controls to control software modifications, protection against unauthorized software alteration, and periodic use of virus detection software to detect infections.

- *Communications security controls,* including installation of security modems/firewalls, use of encryption devices to protect the confidentiality of information, logging of all access attempts (e.g., read, write, execute, create, and delete), establishment of a password management program, protection of dialup access connections, monitoring of users' security practices, periodic review of the audit trail of system activity, reporting invalid access attempts, protection against electromagnetic emanations emitted (by the computers or networks that can be intercepted), cable shielding, and protective devices to process sensitive data.

- *Human resource security controls,* including personnel security policies for those participating in the design and development of software products, training of new employees on their ethical responsibilities, checkout procedures on denying access to departing or transferred personnel/contractors on the computer/network system, training of personnel/contractors on new software development techniques and new risk management processes, and allocation of budget for various training programs.

- *Facility security controls,* including installation of cipher locks to computer/software development areas, implementation of visitor control procedures, use of monitoring devices to detect unauthorized intrusions, periodic inspections to ensure buildings are secured, periodic inspection of fire extinguishers, control of changes in humidity and temperature, providing of emergency lighting, installation of fire and smoke alarms, control of static electricity, protection against power failure and fluctuations, protection against water damage in computer and network areas, and maintaining a clean working environment.

- *Data mechanisms controls*, including protection of disks from magnetism and electromagnetic interference, magnetic media marked with appropriate labels according to level of data sensitivity, protection of master diskettes with write/protect tabs, activation of boot-up passwords on computers, establishment of procedures on files and programs disposal according to sensitivity levels, protection against accidental or intentional lockups in computer or network processing, protection against loss of replicated data, and removal of sensitive residual data appended to smaller modified files.

- *Disaster recovery procedures security controls,* including availability of loaner equipment, a copy of disaster recovery procedures stored off-site, recovery procedures tested at least annually, backup copies of critical files, software packages and original application programs are stored off-site, availability of spare equipment for backup operations, training of selected personnel on disaster recovery responsibilities, and a cost-effective agreement with an off-site facility.

- *Organizational resources security controls,* including implementation of equal employment opportunity and employee incentive programs, establishment of security policies, review of staffing requirements and practices, and review of procurement documents to ensure compliance with security practices and policies for all stages of software development life cycle.

9.2.2 Abbreviated risk method

This section gives examples of vulnerabilities for an abbreviated risk method for a stage of a development life cycle. Management objectives may declare some items listed under a controls category for the checklist risk method as significant vulnerabilities for the abbreviated risk method. As shown in Figure 9.3, hardware alteration is an item under the hardware security controls category. Management objectives declare this item as a significant vulnerability.

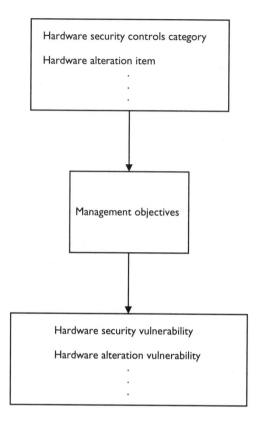

Figure 9.3   Management objectives treat an item of a vulnerability category as the significant vulnerability.

These examples are best illustrated by including them in each threat data sheet, as shown in Chapter 8. Each data sheet shows a short list of vulnerabilities for illustrative purposes. A vulnerability statement must be short and clearly stated. If the vulnerability is ambiguous, it must be clarified. Vulnerabilities in later stages of a life cycle may not be applicable to the first stage.

In reality, the list varies for each threat category in each stage of the life development cycle. Some vulnerabilities may exist in one stage and not in another stage for a threat category. Some vulnerabilities may be applicable to a software product being developed, but not to another product. A test of security controls may be conducted to determine what significant vulnerabilities should be noted and the degree of change in the significance of the vulnerabilities (see

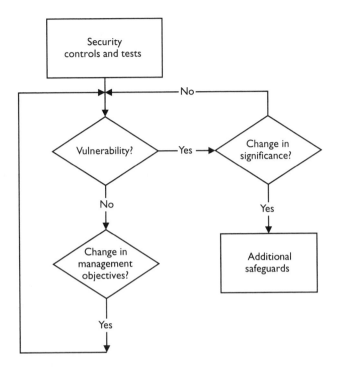

Figure 9.4 Simple security controls and tests flowchart.

Figure 9.4). The test is particularly important regarding security classification and communication encryption of a software development project.

In each data sheet, the list of safeguards already in place will be short for each threat category for illustrative purposes. Impact ratings for each asset will be determined by management objectives on the extent of significant vulnerabilities, what safeguards are already in place, and what additional safeguards are required in each rating category: modification, destruction, and denial of service. Safeguards and impact ratings will be further discussed in Chapter 10.

9.3 Sample data sheets on vulnerabilities

Tables 9.1–9.9 are sample data sheets, taken from Chapter 8 (see Tables 8.1 through 8.9). Safeguards and impact ratings on assets (e.g., hardware and software) will be covered in Chapter 10.

Table 9.1 Sample Data Sheet on Vulnerabilities in the Natural Threat Category on Floods (External)

Threat Data Sheet

Category	Natural threat
Subcategory	External
Type	Floods
Scope	Facility about one mile from Orleans River, which rises with high tides
Average frequency	Twice a year
Historical damage	None

Vulnerabilities

1. Flood warning alarms are deficient
2. Facility does not have an agreement with another facility off-site for backup operations
3. Main computer/network area is primarily located on the first floor in a 15-story building
4. Backup tapes and disk packs are stored in the basement

Safeguards

1.
2.
3.
4.

Impact Ratings	*Modification*	*Destruction*	*Denial of Service*
Hardware			
Software			
Physical			
Human resources			
Office administration			
Data and files			
Network			

Table 9.2   Sample Data Sheet on Vulnerabilities in the Physical Threat Category on Soda and Coffee Spills (Internal)

Threat Data Sheet

Category	Physical threat
Subcategory	Internal
Type	Soda and coffee spills
Scope	Sodas and coffee cups next to desktop computer drives, and keyboard
Average frequency	Ten times a year
Historical damage	Sodas and coffee spilled unto unprotected keyboards

Vulnerabilities

1. Warning signs not to place sodas, coffee cups, and food near computer equipment do not exist

2. Keyboards lack skin covers that users can use while typing

3. Individual work areas do not have separate tables for sodas

4. Sodas and coffee cups placed next to phones

Safeguards

1.

2.

3.

4.

Impact Ratings	*Modification*	*Destruction*	*Denial of Service*
Hardware			
Software			
Physical			
Human resources:			
Office administration			
Data and files			
Network			

Table 9.3 Sample Data Sheet on Vulnerabilities in the Intentional Threat Category on Unauthorized System Access (Insiders)

Threat Data Sheet

Category	Intentional threat
Subcategory	Insiders
Type	Unauthorized system access
Scope	Employees with programming skills who can change file attributes and decipher system files
Average frequency	One incident since a year ago
Historical damage	Operating system crashed, corrupting the directories and files

Vulnerabilities

1. Audit trail is not implemented
2. Security breaks are not recorded on system console
3. Departing employees' system access privileges are not immediately revoked upon departure
4. Individual passwords are not unique
5. File and directory access controls are inadequate

Safeguards

1.
2.
3.
4.

Impact Ratings	*Modification*	*Destruction*	*Denial of Service*
Hardware			
Software			
Physical			
Human resources			
Office administration			
Data and files			
Network			

Table 9.4 Sample Data Sheet on Vulnerabilities in the Intentional Threat Category on Communication Threats (Outsiders)

Threat Data Sheet

Category	Intentional
Subcategory	Outsiders
Type	Communications threats
Scope	Masquerade and denial of service
Average frequency	Four times a year
Historical damage	An outsider pretended to be an authorized user. About three or four authorized users flooded the system with files, records, or messages thus dominating, stopping, or degrading the system

Vulnerabilities

1. Encryption devices/software packages are not installed

2. Security modems/firewalls are not installed

3. Access attempts are not logged

4. Invalid access attempts are not reported

5. Password management program is not implemented

Safeguards

1.

2.

3.

4.

Impact Ratings	*Modification*	*Destruction*	*Denial of Service*
Hardware			
Software			
Physical			
Human resources			
Office administration			
Data and files			
Network			

Table 9.5 Sample Data Sheet on Vulnerabilities in the Unintentional Threat Category on Lack of Disk Management Controls (Inadequate Procedures)

Threat Data Sheet

Category	Unintentional threat
Subcategory	Inadequate procedures
Type	Lack of disk management controls
Scope	Hard disks (removable and nonremovable) and PCMCIA hard cards
Average frequency	Three times a year
Historical damage	High fragmentation of files on a hard disk (magnetic or PCMCIA), resulting in disk crashes

Vulnerabilities

1. High number of fragmented files results in a system crash
2. High number of fragmented files results in damaged operating system, programs, and files that may not be recoverable
3. Fragmented disks are not periodically defragmented
4. Disk management tools are not available

Safeguards

1.
2.
3.
4.

Impact Ratings	*Modification*	*Destruction*	*Denial of Service*
Hardware			
Software			
Physical			
Human resources			
Office administration			
Data and files			
Network			

Table 9.6   Sample Data Sheet on Vulnerabilities in the Unintentional Threat Category on Unintentional Software Developer Error (Inadequate Training)

Threat Data Sheet	
Category	Unintentional threat
Subcategory	Inadequate training
Type	Unintentional software developer error
Scope	Software developer for financial system projects
Average frequency	Ten times a year
Historical damage	Numerous development errors caught at the end of project cycle resulted in project rework, cost overruns, and late delivery of the system due to lack of training on software development

Vulnerabilities

1. Developer does not have appropriate qualifications

2. Developer does not have appropriate background on computer security

3. Developer has received outdated procedures on a software development methodology

4. Management offers a series of training seminars that do not adequately meet the developer's needs

Safeguards

1.

2.

3.

4.

Impact Ratings	*Modification*	*Destruction*	*Denial of Service*
Hardware			
Software			
Physical			
Human resources			
Office administration			
Data and files			
Network			

Table 9.7 Sample Data Sheet on Vulnerabilities in the Unintentional Threat Category on Power Failure/Fluctuation (Ignorance)

Threat Data Sheet

Category	Unintentional threat
Subcategory	Ignorance
Type	Power failure/fluctuation
Scope	Power source for file servers in main computer room
Average frequency	Twice a year
Historical damage	Power failure or fluctuations caused brownouts of the servers

Vulnerabilities

1. Emergency lighting is not adequate
2. The system does not utilize emergency power systems
3. Software modules being developed are not backed up offsite
4. Master power switches are inappropriately identified
5. System personnel are inadequately trained in computer/network emergency shutdown

Safeguards

1.
2.
3.
4.

Impact Ratings	*Modification*	*Destruction*	*Denial of Service*
Hardware			
Software			
Physical			
Human resources			
Office administration			
Data and files			
Network			

Table 9.8   Sample Data Sheet on Vulnerabilities in the Unintentional Threat Category, Such As Inadvertent File Deletion (Ignorance)

Threat Data Sheet	
Category	Unintentional threat
Subcategory	Ignorance
Type	Inadvertent file deletion
Scope	Users/programmers make simple upgrade to software
Average frequency	Three times a year
Historical damage	Important files were inadvertently deleted. File backups were not available

Vulnerabilities

1. Users are inadequately trained in upgrading software packages

2. Users are not assigned deletion file privileges

3. Procedures on disk management are not written

4. Recovery procedures are inadequate

5. Disk is highly fragmented

Safeguards

1.

2.

3.

4.

Impact Ratings	*Modification*	*Destruction*	*Denial of Service*
Hardware			
Software			
Physical			
Human resources			
Office administration			
Data and files			
Network			

Table 9.9   Sample Data Sheet on Vulnerabilities in the Intentional/Unintentional Threat Category, Such As Disgruntled Employees

---

Threat Data Sheet

Category	Unintentional/intentional threat
Subcategory	NA
Type	Disgruntled employees
Scope	Employees who received a notice of layoffs or demotions or who have unsatisfactory relationships with their supervisors
Average frequency	Once since a year ago
Historical damage	A disgruntled employee accidentally deleted all INI files. However, this same employee intentionally changed the internal commands in an operating system

Vulnerabilities

1. Procedures for the termination of accounts are not written

2. Procedures for changing lock/cipher combination are not written

3. User ID/passwords are not changed periodically

4. Terminated employees' access to the software development is inadvertently not revoked

Safeguards

1.

2.

3.

4.

Impact Ratings	*Modification*	*Destruction*	*Denial of Service*
Hardware			
Software			
Physical			
Human resources			
Office administration			
Data and files			
Network			

Chapter 10

Safeguards

SAFEGUARDS ARE mechanisms used to counter the weaknesses of the vulnerabilities in the systems. Countering a vulnerability reduces its weaknesses to a more economically acceptable level of risk. Existing safeguards must be identified after security controls are tested. If safeguards do not exist or are inadequate, they should be evaluated for their cost-effectiveness and recommended for implementation.

Depending on the risks to which a system is vulnerable, some safeguards are significant, others are insignificant or inapplicable. The more complex the system becomes, the more likely the risks to the system will be complex and compounded. Complex sets of risks will require complex sets of safeguards. Like vulnerabilities, safeguards may exist in one software development stage and not in another.

Safeguards that are applicable to most systems may be used as standard templates. Similar to customized assets, security threats, and security controls, the templates can be tailored to suit a particular situation of a project or a specific stage of the development life cycle. The templates are repeatable processes and should be flexible enough to allow changes, for technology evolves quicker than the safeguards to counter the vulnerabilities.

To ensure the templates are periodically updated, management objectives should be established or reviewed as technology significantly changes. The objectives should consider the identification of safeguards (as well as threats) as an important part of a risk management program. Without safeguard identification, it is not possible to reduce the vulnerabilities to more acceptable risk levels or determine what additional safeguards are required.

Examples of templates include a list of questions on safeguards for a particular security control for the checklist risk method. Also included is a list of safeguards grouped under a security control for the abbreviated risk method.

Identifying safeguards for each stage of a software development life cycle (see Figure 10.1) is the fourth step in applying risk management processes to software processes.

This step overcomes the deficiencies of safeguards in software engineering models (see Chapter 3). Two other deficiencies are noted. In the security arena (see Chapter 5), identified safeguards are the same for each stage of the cycle. Safeguards are not treated as a category in the software risk management theories discussed in Chapter 6. Risk management techniques are one aspect of a safeguard. They do not include another aspect of the safeguard: corrective devices.

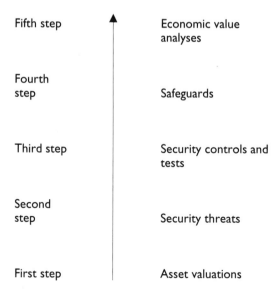

Figure 10.1   Safeguards is the fourth step in risk management processes.

To identify what safeguards are already in place and what additional safeguards are required, one should keep in mind that requirements (see Figure 10.2)for safeguards differ among personal computer workstations, network systems, minicomputers, and mainframes. The differences in safeguards requirements are attributed, in part, to unique characteristics and vulnerabilities in the systems used to develop software products. Safeguard requirements for one stage of a software development process differ from safeguard requirements in another stage. The degree of differences depends on the complexity of the projects.

10.1 Two safeguard scenarios

Examples of existing safeguards already in place and additional safeguards to be implemented are provided in two commuter train scenarios. The first scenario

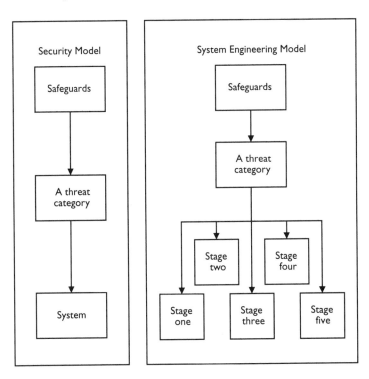

Figure 10.2 Safeguards in a system are redefined to include safeguards for any stage of a development life cycle.

shows safeguards exist when falling leaves increase the vulnerability of the train to slippery tracks. The second scenario shows how an inspection team finds vulnerabilities and recommends safeguards to reduce these vulnerabilities.

10.1.1 Falling leaves and high speed

When commuter trains are traveling at high speed in autumn, they are vulnerable to accidents with the threat of excessive leaves falling on the tracks. At a certain high-speed level, the trains can begin to slide on tracks.

To safeguard the passengers from potential accidents, the trains must travel at slower speeds. Notices of trains traveling at slower speeds are posted at all train stations. This indicates that this safeguard has been implemented. The safeguard exists and is adequate—according to standards set by management objectives on a security policy. No additional safeguards are needed.

The costs of implementing this safeguard countering the vulnerabilities are much less than the costs of reimbursing the accident victims. The safeguard not only includes procedures and actions, but also safety devices (in train engineer's work area) and techniques (of slowing down the train in a safe manner).

10.1.2 Defective safety device

Let's suppose an inspection team during a routine inspection discovers a defective safety device in the engineer's work area. The inspection team mandates the repair or replacement of the device. The train on a particular run is taken to the repair shop.

As a result, the passengers are inconvenienced by an inadequate number of seats during rush hours while the device is being repaired or replaced. Passengers call the transit company to complain. This can keep the company telephone operators busy, who may work overtime to log the complaints.

For this scenario, additional safeguards are recommended, such as:

- A backup device in the train engineer's work area;
- Procedures requiring the engineer to periodically inspect safety devices and notify immediately the inspection team of the potential problems;
- Procedures to repair and replace the device at off-hours.

These examples give some possibilities of countering the weaknesses of the vulnerabilities of the breakdown in a safety device and reduce the vulnerabilities to more economically acceptable levels.

10.2 **Safeguards**

The concepts of checklist risk method and abbreviated risk method, as discussed in Chapter 5, can be applied to safeguards in any one stage of development life cycle. The safeguards in the checklist are easier to group than those for the abbreviated method. The abbreviated risk method lists significant safeguards for each threat data sheet. These safeguards are recommended to counter the vulnerabilities.

10.2.1 **Checklist risk method**

This section gives examples of safeguards under various categories. The categories in a security arena may differ from those categories for systems engineering models. Safeguard categories in the checklist risk method are relatively simple. Management objectives should consider one of the following three options in developing safeguard categories:

- Safeguard categories as simple as "yes" or "no" responses to questions on security controls and tests.
- A checklist of safeguard categories should be established that bear little resemblance to security controls and tests.
- Safeguard categories should be established that reflect a mix of two options.

However, for illustrative purposes, the categories for safeguards are simple responses to the questions in the checklist. For example, the following are safeguard categories that are simple responses to items under security controls and tests discussed in Chapter 9:

- Hardware;
- Software;
- Communications;
- Human resources;
- Facility;
- Data mechanisms;
- Disaster recovery;
- Organizational resources.

10.2.2 Abbreviated risk method

This section gives examples of safeguards for an abbreviated risk method for a stage of a development life cycle. Management objectives may declare some items listed under a controls category for the checklist risk method as significant safeguards for the abbreviated risk method (see Figure 10.3).

These examples are best illustrated by including them in each threat data sheet as shown in Chapter 9. Each data sheet shows a short list of safeguards for illustrative purposes. A safeguard requirement must be short and clearly stated. If the safeguard is ambiguous, it must be clarified. Like vulnerabilities, safeguards in later stages of a life cycle may not be applicable to the first stage.

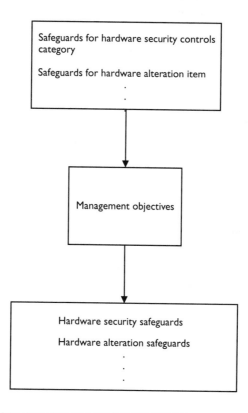

Figure 10.3 Management objectives treat selected items of a security controls category as significant safeguards.

In reality, the list varies for each threat category in each stage of the development life cycle. Some safeguards may exist in one stage and not in another stage for a threat category.

Likewise, additional safeguards may be required in one stage and not in another stage. The significance of these safeguards may become more or less when management objectives on security policies change or when there is a change of management, with a different philosophy on security policies.

In each threat data sheet, the safeguard list will be short for each threat category for illustrative purposes. Impact ratings for each asset are grouped into three impact categories: modification, destruction, and denial of service. The ratings assigned to each asset category will be determined by management objectives on the following:

- The extent of significant vulnerabilities;
- What safeguards are already in place;
- How complex it is to activate existing safeguards;
- How much it costs to recommend alternatives of additional safeguards;
- How much it costs to implement selected alternatives;
- What additional safeguards are recommended or required.

10.3 Sample data sheets on safeguards

Tables 10.1–10.9 are sample data sheets, taken from Chapter 9 (see Tables 9.1 through 9.9). Safeguards and impact ratings on assets (e.g., hardware and software) are included.

Impact categories cover modification, destruction, and denial of service. Blank columns are interpreted as not applicable. They are restricted to three for this book. In real-life situations, there may be more than three impact categories.

For easier reference, the following give examples of which data sheets have impact ratings in one impact category and which other data sheets have ratings in more than one categories. The impact ratings are arbitrary and for illustrative purposes only. These ratings may differ from the ratings specified by management objectives in practice.

One impact category exists in the natural threat category on floods (Table 10.1), one in the intentional threat category on communication threats

(Table 10.4), one in the unintentional threat category on power failure/fluctuation (Table 10.7), and another for unintentional threats, such as inadvertent file deletion (Table 10.8). The first table is concerned with the destruction impact category and the rest with the denial of service category.

Two impact categories are provided in the physical threat category on soda and coffee spills (Table 10.2), in the intentional threat category on unauthorized system access (Tale 10.3), in the unintentional threat category on lack of disk management controls (Table 10.5), and in the unintentional threat category on unintentional software developer error (Table 10.6).

The first and third tables are concerned with the destruction and denial of service categories. The second and fourth tables show modification and denial of service categories.

The three impact categories of modification, destruction, and denial of service are found in the unintentional/intentional category, such as disgruntled employees (Table 10.9).

Table 10.1 Sample Data Sheet on Safeguards to Counter Vulnerabilities in the Natural Threat Category on Floods (External)

Threat Data Sheet

Category	Natural threat
Subcategory	External
Type	Floods
Scope	Facility about one mile from Orleans River, which rises with high tides
Average frequency	Twice a year
Historical damage	None

Vulnerabilities

1. Flood warning alarms are deficient
2. Facility does not have an agreement with another facility off-site for backup operations
3. Main computer/network area is primarily located on the first floor in a 15-story building
4. Backup tapes and disk packs are stored in the basement

Safeguards

1. Install water sensors
2. Prepare a backup agreement with an off-site facility
3. Move main computer/network area to upper floors
4. Move backup tapes and disk packs to an off-site facility

Impact Ratings	Modification	Destruction	Denial of Service
Hardware		Medium	
Software		Medium	
Physical		Medium	
Human resources		NA	
Office administration		Medium	
Data and files		Medium	
Network		Medium	

Table 10.2   Sample Data Sheet on Safeguards to Counter Vulnerabilities in the Physical Threat Category on Soda and Coffee Spills (Internal)

Threat Data Sheet	
Category	Physical threat
Subcategory	Internal
Type	Soda and coffee spills
Scope	Sodas and coffee cups next to desktop computer drives, keyboard
Average frequency	Ten times a year
Historical damage	Sodas and coffee spilled on to unprotected keyboards

Vulnerabilities

1. Warning signs not to place sodas, coffee cups, and food near computer equipment do not exist
2. Keyboards lack skin covers that the users can use while typing
3. Individual work areas does not have separate tables for sodas, coffee cups, and food
4. Sodas and coffee cups placed next to phones

Safeguards

1. Post warning signs not to place drinks/food near computer equipment
2. Cover keyboards with transparent skins
3. Provide separate tables for drinks/food away from computer equipment
4. Issue periodic memorandums to employees not to place drinks near phones

Impact Ratings	*Modification*	*Destruction*	*Denial of Service*
Hardware		Medium	Medium
Software		Low	Low
Physical		Medium	NA
Human resources		NA	NA
Office administration		Medium	NA
Data and files		Low	Low
Network		High	High

Table 10.3 Sample Data Sheet on Safeguards to Counter Vulnerabilities in the Intentional Threat Category on Unauthorized System Access (Insiders)

Threat Data Sheet

Category	Intentional threat
Subcategory	Insiders
Type	Unauthorized system access
Scope	Employees with programming skills who can change file attributes and decipher system files
Average frequency	One incident since a year ago
Historical damage	Operating system crashed, corrupting the directories and files

Vulnerabilities

1. Audit trail is not implemented

2. Security breaks are not logged on system console

3. Departing employees' system access privileges are not immediately revoked upon departure

4. Individual passwords are not unique or contain few characters

Safeguards

1. Implement audit trail

2. Activate the logging of security breaks on system console

3. Revoke departing employees' system access

4. Suppress passwords on terminals

5. Implement minimal password verification

Impact Ratings	Modification	Destruction	Denial of Service
Hardware	NA		NA
Software	Medium		Medium
Physical	NA		NA
Human resources	NA		NA
Office administration	NA		NA
Data and files	Medium		Medium
Network	NA		NA

Table 10.4   Sample Data Sheet on Safeguards to Counter Vulnerabilities in the Intentional Threat Category on Communication Threats (Outsiders)

Threat Data Sheet	
Category	Intentional threat
Subcategory	Outsiders
Type	Communications threats
Scope	Masquerade and denial of service
Average frequency	Four times a year
Historical damage	An outsider pretended to be an authorized user. About three or four authorized users flooded the system with files, records, or messages thus dominating, stopping, or degrading the system

Vulnerabilities

1. Encryption devices/software packages are not installed

2. Security modems are not installed

3. Access attempts are not logged

4. Invalid access attempts are not reported

5. Password management program is not implemented

Safeguards

1. Install encryption devices/software packages

2. Activate the logging of access attempts

3. Report invalid access attempts

4. Implement password management program

Impact Ratings	*Modification*	*Destruction*	*Denial of Service*
Hardware			NA
Software			Medium
Physical			NA
Human resources			NA
Office administration			NA
Data and files			Medium
Network			Medium

Table 10.5 Sample Data Sheet on Safeguards to Counter Vulnerabilities in the Unintentional Threat Category on Lack of Disk Management Controls (Inadequate Procedures)

Threat Data Sheet

Category	Unintentional threat
Subcategory	Inadequate procedures
Type	Lack of disk management controls
Scope	Hard disks (removable and nonremoveable) and PCMCIA hard cards)
Average frequency	Three times a year
Historical damage	High fragmentation of files on a hard disk (magnetic or PCMCIA) resulting in disk crashes

Vulnerabilities

1. High number of fragmented files results in a system crash

2. High number of fragmented files results in damaged operating system, programs, and files that may not be recoverable

3. Fragmented disks are not periodically defragmented

4. Disk management tools are not available

Safeguards

1. Defragment the hard disks on a periodic basis

2. Purchase disk management tools

3. Expand current security policy on the use of disk management tools

4. Implement disaster/recovery plan for periodic testing

Impact Ratings	*Modification*	*Destruction*	*Denial of Service*
Hardware		Medium	Medium
Software		High	High
Physical		NA	NA
Human resources		NA	NA
Office administration		NA	NA
Data and files		High	High
Network		Medium	Medium

Table 10.6   Sample Data Sheet on Safeguards to Counter Vulnerabilities in the Unintentional Threat Category on Unintentional Software Developer Error (Inadequate Training)

Threat Data Sheet

Category	Unintentional threat
Subcategory	Inadequate training
Type	Unintentional software developer error
Scope	Software developer for financial system projects
Average frequency	200 times a year
Historical damage	Numerous development errors caught at the end of project cycle resulted in project rework, cost overruns, and late delivery of the system due to lack of training on software development

Vulnerabilities

1. Developer does not have appropriate qualifications

2. Developer does not have appropriate background on computer security

3. Developer has received outdated procedures on a software development methodology

4. Management offers a series of training seminars that do not adequately meet the developer's needs

Safeguards

1. Enroll developer in training courses to improve or gain qualifications

2. Enroll developer in computer security training

3. Update or rewrite procedures on software development methodology

4. Review developer's needs and recommend more appropriate training seminars

Impact Ratings	*Modification*	*Destruction*	*Denial of Service*
Hardware	NA		NA
Software	Medium		High
Physical	NA		NA
Human resources	Medium		Medium
Office administration	NA		NA
Data and files	Medium		Medium
Network	NA		NA

Table 10.7 Sample Data Sheet on Safeguards to Counter Vulnerabilities in the Unintentional Threat Category on Power Failure/Fluctuation (Ignorance)

Threat Data Sheet

Category	Unintentional threat
Subcategory	Ignorance
Type	Power failure/fluctuation
Scope	Power source for file servers in main computer room
Average frequency	Twice a year

Historical damage: Power failure or fluctuations caused brownouts of the servers

Vulnerabilities

1. Emergency lighting is not adequate
2. The system does not utilizes emergency power systems
3. Software modules being developed are not backed up offsite
4. Master power switches are inappropriately identified
5. System personnel are inadequately trained in computer/network emergency shutdown

Safeguards

1. Periodically inspect emergency lighting
2. Connect emergency power systems to the system
3. Arrange an off-site facility to store backed up software modules
4. Label master power switches
5. Provide system personnel with training in emergency shutdown

Impact Ratings	*Modification*	*Destruction*	*Denial of Service*
Hardware			Medium
Software			Medium
Physical			NA
Human resources			NA
Office administration			NA
Data and files			Medium
Network			Low

Table 10.8   Sample Data Sheet on Safeguards to Counter Vulnerabilities in the Unintentional Threat Category, Such As Inadvertent File Deletion (ignorance)

Threat Data Sheet	
Category	Unintentional threat
Subcategory	Ignorance
Type	Inadvertent file deletion
Scope	Users/programmers make simple upgrade to software
Average frequency	Three times a year
Historical damage	Important files were inadvertently deleted. File backups were not available

Vulnerabilities

1. Users are inadequately trained in upgrading software packages

2. Users are inadvertently assigned deletion file privileges

3. Procedures on disk management are not written

4. Recovery procedures are inadequate

5. Disk is highly fragmented

Safeguards

1. Provide users with training to upgrade software packages

2. Lock out users from file deletion privileges

3. Prepare procedures on disk management and recovery procedures

4. Periodically defragment the disks

Impact Ratings	Modification	Destruction	Denial of Service
Hardware			NA
Software			High
Physical			NA
Human resources			NA
Office administration			NA
Data and files			Medium
Network			Medium

Table 10.9 Sample Data Sheet on Safeguards to Counter Vulnerabilities in the Unintentional/Intentional Category, Such As Disgruntled Employees

Threat Data Sheet	
Category	Unintentional/intentional threat
Subcategory	NA
Type	Disgruntled employees
Scope	Employees who received a notice of layoffs or demotions or who have unsatisfactory relationships with their supervisors
Average frequency	Once since a year ago
Historical damage	A disgruntled employee accidentally deleted all .ini files. However, this same employee intentionally changed the internal commands in an operating system

Vulnerabilities

1. Procedures for the termination of accounts are not written

2. Procedures for changing lock/cipher combination are not written

3. User ID/passwords are not changed periodically

4. Terminated employees' access to software development project is inadvertently not revoked

Safeguards

1. Prepare procedures to terminate user accounts

2. Prepare procedures to change lock/cipher combination on a periodic basis

3. Change periodically user ID/passwords

4. Revoke terminated employees' access to software development project

Impact Ratings	*Modification*	*Destruction*	*Denial of Service*
Hardware	Low	Medium	Medium
Software	Low	Medium	Medium
Physical	NA	NA	NA
Human resources	NA	NA	NA
Office administration	NA	NA	NA
Data and files	Medium	Medium	Medium
Network	NA	NA	NA

Chapter 11

Economic analysis

I N RISK ASSESSMENT, economic analysis is concerned with relative values (rather than with absolute numbers) of asset loss impacts on the software development project. This is known as economic value analysis.

Economic value analysis consists of three main areas. One area focuses on computing mathematical values of implementing additional security controls and safeguards to reduce the risks to acceptable levels. The second area of economic analysis looks at the savings justification of implementing the controls and safeguards. The third area, the most important part, is the ROI in each stage of the software development process for each threat category. This chapter gives more information on these three areas of economic value analysis.

11.1 Mathematical values

Before we discuss the use of mathematical values in economic analysis to manage risks, software development process management and impact ratings are briefly covered. After this, discussions on risk prioritization rules and probabilistic algorithms follow.

11.1.1 Software engineering risk management

One good example of development process management is the software engineering risk management approach as suggested by Dale Walter Karolak [1]. Using this approach, Karolak divides the software category into process and product for 10 software risk factors.

The following risk factors are identified as software process categories. Each factor is briefly defined:

- *Organization*: The maturity level of the organization structure, communications, functions and leadership;
- *Estimation*: Risks of inaccurate estimations of the resources, schedules, and costs of developing software;
- *Monitoring*: Risks of identifying problems with milestones, tracking costs, and scheduling;
- *Development methodology*: Risks of using the methods to develop software;
- *Tools*: Risks of using software tools to develop software;
- *Risk culture*: Risks in management decision-making process;
- *Personnel*: The ability to use the software development methods, tools and the knowledge to develop software.

The following risk factors are identified as software product categories. The risks of the product are considered once the product is delivered to the end user.

- Usability;
- Correctness;
- Reliability.

In addition, Karolak divides software risk elements into technical, cost, and schedule for each risk factor. Karolak suggests an assignment of a low, medium, or high rating to each technical, cost, and schedule risk element for each factor.

Of the seven risk factors identified as software process categories, the cost and schedule risk elements are rated high for the following five:

- Organization;
- Estimation;
- Monitoring;
- Development methodology;
- Personnel.

For the remaining two risk factors, the technical risk element is rated high for the risk culture risk factor, and all three risk elements (technical, cost, and schedule) are rated medium for the tools risk factor.

To better understand the role of software risk factors in risk management activities, Karolak identifies six risk activities:

- Identification;
- Strategy and planning;
- Assessment;
- Mitigation/avoidance;
- Reporting;
- Prediction.

For each activity, Karolak provides sample metrics questions that are measured on a probabilistic scale from 0 to 1.

Not all questions are applicable to each risk activity. Important in economic analysis are the assessment and mitigation/avoidance activities. As shown in Figure 11.1, more metric questions on development methodology and monitoring risk factors are applicable to the mitigation/avoidance activity than to the assessment activity. The total numbers of metric questions asked are the same and are found within the parenthesis next to the risk factor headers. As stated before, development methodology and monitoring risk factors are both software process categories.

On the other hand, Figures 11.2 and 11.3 show that more metric questions on the estimation, tools, correctness, and reliability risk factors are applicable to the assessment activity than to the mitigation/avoidance activity. The total number of questions for the estimation and tool risk factors are 7 and 9, respectively. The total number of questions for the correctness and reliability risk factors are 9 and 12, respectively.

Software categories are mixed. Estimation and tools risk factors are software process categories. Correctness and reliability risk factors are software product categories.

Risk Activities	Comparison of Total Metric Questions Between Risk Factors	
	Development Methodology (7)	Monitoring (7)
Assessment	2	3
Mitigation/Avoidance	6	7

Figure 11.1   Total metric questions are compared between development methodology and monitoring risk factors for two risk activities: assessment and mitigation/avoidance. (*After:* [1].)

Risk Activities	Comparison of Total Metric Questions Between Risk Factors	
	Estimation (7)	Tools (9)
Assessment	6	6
Mitigation/Avoidance	4	1

Figure 11.2   Total metric questions are compared between the estimation and tool risk factors for two risk activities: assessment and mitigation/avoidance. (*After:* [1].)

	Comparison of Total Metric Questions Between Risk Factors	
Risk Activities	Correctness (9)	Reliability (12)
Assessment	9	11
Mitigation/Avoidance	6	5

Figure 11.3   Total metric questions are compared between the correctness and reliability risk factors for two risk activities: assessment and mitigation/avoidance. (*After:* [1].)

The number of metric questions concerned with organization risk factors are the same for both the assessment and mitigation/avoidance activities. Although seven questions are asked, only four questions are applicable to both activities. One question applies to only to the assessment activity. The other question applies to the mitigation/avoidance activity. The remaining three questions are not applicable.

Metric questions are subjective and cannot be considered as "repeatable processes." Yet, Karolak makes a good point that development methodology and monitoring are important risk factors in mitigating or avoiding the risks. This book considers organization, development methodology, and monitoring risk factors as intangible threats. Risks associated with these factors sometimes can be converted into mathematical values.

11.1.2   Impact ratings

This section includes two examples of impact ratings. One example covers the disgruntled employees threat. The other example discusses briefly the unintentional software developer error threat (which is considered an intangible threat in development methodology). Then, discussions on prioritization rules and probability algorithms are covered.

Disgruntled employees threat

Disgruntled employees are a potential threat to the software development project in any stage of the life cycle. For example, they have received a notice of layoff or demotion. They also have unsatisfactory relationships with their supervisors.

Disgruntled employees can modify files, destroy software, or deny service to others. They can sabotage, steal, misuse computer resources, access the system and mess up software modules, and flood the system with messages that tie up the resources. They also can alter hardware, infect the systems with malicious viruses, make changes to the operating systems, and deny the service to authorized users.

Table 11.1 shows vulnerabilities of a disgruntled employee who accidentally deleted all .ini files. These files are needed to run various Windows application programs. The same employee intentionally changed the internal commands in an operating system. The changes in internal commands confused other users who were authorized to use operating system commands. For example, the change in the spelling of the Del command to a nonsensical JLO command cannot be easily "interpreted" by the authorized user. The user was denied service.

To counter these vulnerabilities, additional safeguards are recommended. Impact ratings for seven assets are given for all three impact categories: modification, destruction, and denial of service. Not applicable ratings are assigned to physical, human resources, office administration, and network assets in three impact categories.

Impact ratings for hardware and software assets in the modification category are lower than those in the destruction and denial of service categories. The disgruntled employee is not an engineer or a programmer, but can destroy a software product with the Del command, thus denying the service to others. Impact ratings for data and files are the same in all three categories. The disgruntled employee can modify, destroy, and deny the service to other users.

Unintentional software developer errors

Unintentional software developer errors are a potential to the software development project in any stage of the life cycle. Numerous development errors were caught at the end of the project cycle. This resulted in project rework, cost overruns, and late delivery of the system. Training on software development was inadequate.

Table 11.2 shows the vulnerabilities of developers who contributed to cumulative errors at the end of the project cycle. The developers do not have appropriate qualifications and background on computer security. The develop-

Table 11.1   Sample Data Sheet on Safeguards to Counter Vulnerabilities in the Unintentional/ Intentional Threat Category, Such As Disgruntled Employees

Threat Data Sheet	
Category	Unintentional/intentional threat
Subcategory	NA
Type	Disgruntled employees
Scope	Employees who received a notice of layoffs or demotions or who have unsatisfactory relationships with their supervisors
Average frequency	Once since a year ago
Historical damage	A disgruntled employee accidentally deleted all .ini files. However, this same employee intentionally changed internal commands in an operating system to unrecognizable words

Vulnerabilities

1. Procedures for the termination of accounts are not written

2. Procedures for changing lock/cipher combination are not written

3. User ID/passwords are not changed periodically

4. Terminated employees' access to software development project is inadvertently not revoked

Safeguards

1. Prepare procedures to terminate user accounts

2. Prepare procedures to change lock/cipher combination on a periodic basis

3. Change periodically user ID/passwords

4. Revoke terminated employees' access to software development project

Impact ratings	*Modification*	*Destruction*	*Denial of service*
Hardware	Low	Medium	Medium
Software	Low	Medium	Medium
Physical	NA	NA	NA
Human resources	NA	NA	NA
Office administration	NA	NA	NA
Data and files	Medium	Medium	Medium
Network	NA	NA	NA

Table 11.2 Sample Data Sheet on Safeguards to Counter Vulnerabilities in the Unintentional Threat Category on Unintentional Software Developer Error (Inadequate Training)

Threat Data Sheet

Category	Unintentional threat
Subcategory	Inadequate training
Type	Unintentional software developer error
Scope	Software developer for financial system projects
Average frequency	Ten times a year
Historical damage	Numerous development errors caught at the end of the project cycle resulted in project rework, cost overruns, and late delivery of the system due to lack of training on software development

Vulnerabilities

1. Developer does not have appropriate qualifications

2. Developer does not have appropriate background on computer security

3. Developer has received outdated procedures on a software development methodology

4. Management offers a series of training seminars that do not adequately meet the developer's needs

Safeguards

1. Enroll developer in training courses to improve or gain qualifications

2. Enroll developer in computer security training

3. Update or rewrite procedures on software development methodology

4. Review developer's needs and recommend more appropriate training seminars

Impact Ratings	Modification	Destruction	Denial of Service
Hardware	NA		NA
Software	Medium		High
Physical	NA		NA
Human resources	Medium		Medium
Office administration	NA		NA
Data and files	Medium		Medium
Network	NA		NA

ers also have received outdated procedures on a software development methodology. Management has offered a series of training seminars, but these seminars do not adequately meet the needs of the developers.

To counter these vulnerabilities, additional safeguards are recommended. Impact ratings for the seven assets are given only in two of three impact categories: modification and denial of service. Not applicable ratings are assigned to hardware, physical, office administration, and network assets.

Impact rating for software in the modification category is lower than for that in the denial of service. It is highly likely numerous errors will result in denial of service. It is less likely that numerous errors will modify the software. Impact ratings for human resources as well as data and files are the same in two categories.

11.1.3   Risk prioritization rules

Threat data sheets not covered for other categories in Chapter 10 may also show the same rating assignments for one or more of three impact categories: modification, destruction, and denial of service. To determine which threat category has a higher priority over another threat category, some kind of prioritization rules need to be established.

These rules should be flexible enough to allow changes in the prioritization of threat categories with the same impact ratings for all assets in any stage of the development life cycle. One possibility is the quantitative adaptation of the analytical hierarchy process (AHP) as proposed by Ruthberg and Fisher [2].

Analytical hierarchy process

The AHP process has been widely used by computer auditors in different types of decision problems. The auditors use this process to

- Develop the hierarchy of attributes of the problem;
- Identify the relative importance of attributes;
- Obtain the measure of the relative performance of each alternative on each element of the hierarchy.

It is claimed that AHP is more effective than subjective judgment and personal preference, and also the annual loss expectancy (ALE) formula. The judgment method allows the auditor to associate intellectually his knowledge and past experience to determine the magnitude of risks of subsystems. This method is not a "transferable skill" and is unique to each auditor. For this reason, subjective judgment is not a candidate for a template and, thus, is not a repeatable process.

11.1.4 Probability algorithms

This section looks at one example of a probability algorithm. It is called annual loss expectancy (ALE). This algorithm is widely used, especially in insurance industries and other business entities (such as security and disaster planning) to predict the costs of expected annual loss.

Annual loss expectancy

Various forms of ALE algorithms have been used to represent low, medium, and high ratings, such as the following:

- Simple absolute probabilistic values of .333, .667, and 1;
- Computed absolute probabilistic values of .003, .033, and .333;
- Variable probabilities values of 0 through .299, .3 through .599, and .6 through 1;
- Probabilistic values as weighting factors.

According to Ruthberg and Fisher [2], ALE describes a system risk in simplistic terms and consists of two main components:

- Frequency of occurrence;
- Loss per occurrence.

The frequency of occurrence of a problem can be represented by a probability. It is important to know what kind of loss will result from a system problem. Subtracting loss per occurrence from frequency of occurrence gives the formula of annual loss expectancy, as follows:

Frequency of Occurrence − Loss per Occurrence = Annual Loss Expectancy

This formula may be quantified in dollar values.

The advantage of providing risks of expected loss in dollars is that one can see the savings realized before and after additional security controls and safeguards are implemented. The savings in dollars are needed to determine the ROI of the ratio between the costs and savings of implementing the controls and safeguards.

The disadvantage is that the risks of expected loss in dollars may be estimates and do not reflect the true cost replacements of the assets. The costs of the equipment can change over a period of time. The employees get annual increases in salaries. Tax laws change. The actual costs of older software versions may not be available.

Ruthberg and Fisher's formula is not suitable for the abbreviated risk method. It does not take into consideration the ALE of each asset in each stage of a development life cycle project.

To compute the ALE (in dollar values) of each asset for each threat category, the assets and threat categories should be arranged in a matrix format. The threat categories could be listed on the left side of the matrix with the assets across the top. The ALE for all asset categories for each threat categories could be listed on the right side of the matrix. The ALE for all threat categories for each asset categories could be placed across the bottom of the matrix. Management objectives can determine the formula used in computing the ALEs.

ALEs can be revised to reflect the savings in implementing existing and new safeguards and security controls. The matrix with original ALEs is known as the original risk method matrix (see Table 11.3). The matrix with revised ALEs is known as the revised risk method matrix.

One example of an ALE matrix formula is the use of probability as weighting factors. Management objectives need to be established to determine appropriate weighting factors for the complexity and type of software product suite to be developed throughout its life cycle. The weighting factors could differ for each stage of life cycle development.

Multiplying a weighting factor to the dollar value of each asset for each threat category can be tedious by hand, especially for a complex development process in each stage of a life cycle process. It is even more tedious to recalculate risk weights when threats and vulnerabilities change frequently during development process. To make the tasks of computing weighted ALEs easier, a personal computer software package is recommended.

11.2 Savings justification

Only moderate and high risks of the threats are included in the savings justification sheets for the abbreviated risk method. The savings after successful implementation of the safeguards should result in reducing the risks to more acceptable levels. Management objectives should specify which risk levels are acceptable and which levels are unacceptable.

Table 11.3 Sample Matrix Format for the Original Risk Method Matrix

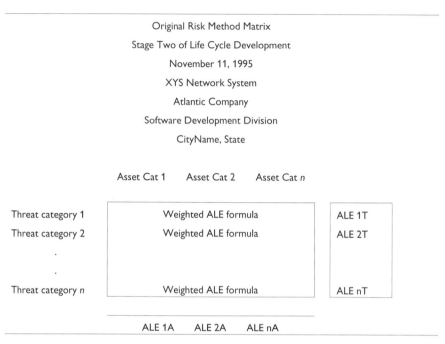

Original Risk Method Matrix

Stage Two of Life Cycle Development

November 11, 1995

XYS Network System

Atlantic Company

Software Development Division

CityName, State

	Asset Cat 1	Asset Cat 2	Asset Cat n	
Threat category 1		Weighted ALE formula		ALE 1T
Threat category 2		Weighted ALE formula		ALE 2T
.				
.				
Threat category n		Weighted ALE formula		ALE nT
	ALE 1A	ALE 2A	ALE nA	

Savings are determined by comparing the expected values for each asset between the original risk analysis matrix and the revised risk analysis matrix. For a software development process project, safeguards as well as savings differ from one stage to another in a development life cycle.

Management objectives on safeguards can change over a period of time as technology evolves and organizational policies are updated. Safeguards identified as significant in one computer environment (e.g., personal computers) may become insignificant in another environment (e.g., a client/server platform). Likewise, safeguards identified as insignificant in one computer environment (e.g., computers at a great distance from the border of an unfriendly nation) may become significant in another environment (e.g., computers at a close proximity to the border).

Table 11.4 shows savings in implementing additional safeguards and security controls for various threat categories in one stage of the life cycle. One safeguard can be used to counter the vulnerabilities of one or more than one threat categories. For example, the addition of a password control safeguard is used to counter the vulnerabilities of unauthorized leakage, unauthorized system access, and other threats. The addition of a contingency plan safeguard is used, partially, to counter the vulnerabilities of system failure, unauthorized hardware alteration, and other threats. The addition of auto network backup is a good safeguard suggestion to counter the threats of improper data replication.

Implementation costs are included. First, it costs $200 of man hours to implement the password control safeguard. The costs would be higher if a software package is needed to improve security features. Second, it costs $300 to prepare, write, and distribute copies of a contingency plan. The more complex the software development project and the computer system are, the higher the costs of implementing the contingency plan become. Third, it costs $150 of man hours to install an auto network backup to counter the vulnerabilities of improper data replications. Fourth, it costs $150 to install antivirus mechanisms and train the users to detect unauthorized software alteration. This includes both man hours and software products. The bottom of the table shows grand saving totals and grand costs, as well as total return on investments, safeguard priorities, and impacts of savings on other safeguards. Safeguard priorities are high. If the priorities differ for each safeguard, a separate column would need to be added to the table. For example, management objectives would give high priorities to contingency plan and auto network backup safeguards and medium priority to an antivirus mechanism safeguard.

11.3 Return on investments

Discussions on return on investments have been inadequately covered or not covered at all for some software engineering models in previous chapters. Several ways of computing total return on investment (ROI) are available.

One example is a total return on investment as the ratio of total costs to total savings. This is used in the abbreviated risk method and in the comprehensive risk method. It is not used in the checklist risk method.

Table 11.4 arbitrarily shows a grand total of ROI of 1:78 for illustrative purposes. However, the ROI for each safeguard to be implemented is, obviously, a better indicator of how well (arbitrarily) the implemented safeguard can return the investment than the grand ROI.

The ROIs for the safeguard are as follows:

- Password control   1:75
- Contingency plan   1:83

Table 11.4 The Savings Justification Sheet Gives a Total Return on Investment for a Network System

Savings Justification Sheet
Stage Two of Life Cycle Development
November 11,1995
XYZ Network System
Atlantic Company
Software Development Division
CityName, State

Safeguards	Threat categories	Savings	Costs
Password control	Unauthorized leakage	$10,000	
	Unauthorized system access	5,000	
	Subtotal	$15,000	$200
Contingency plan	System failure	$20,000	
	Unauthorized hardware alteration	5,000	
	Subtotal	$25,000	$300
Auto network backup	Improper data replication	$12,000	
	Subtotal	$12,000	$150
Antivirus mechanisms	Unauthorized software alternation	$10,000	
	Subtotal	$10,000	$150

Grand total: $62,000,Grand costs: $800,Total return on investments: 1:78
Priorities: high for all safeguards,Impacts on other safeguards: none

- Auto network backup   1:80
- Antivirus mechanisms   1:67

These ROIs probably will not reflect the ROIs in real-life situations. They may be lower or higher. These ROIs are positive when costs are less than savings.

The higher the costs are, the lower the ROIs will be. If the costs equal the savings, an ROI does not exist. If ROIs are nearly the same or if the management objectives specify otherwise, prioritization rules should be developed.

Negative ROIs occur when the costs are greater than the savings. When the ROIs are negative, lower alternative costs of implementing the safeguards or higher alternative savings of improved annual loss expectancy should be considered. Negative ROIs are rare.

The costs are based on actual dollar values. They may or may not be amortized (e.g., two or five years). Management objectives should specify which categories of costs can be amortized and which cannot be amortized (e.g., straight annual costs only). If a safeguard is not implemented within a reasonable specified time, the costs should be increased to include the cost value of nonimplementation. Increased costs can lower an ROI for the safeguard. A table should be developed to calculate lower values of ROIs over a period of time.

It is obvious that it is easier to measure ROIs with costs than benefits. Some benefits can be quantified, others are unquantifiable. If they cannot be quantified, subjective probabilistic values should be used.

If a safeguard is not implemented within a reasonable time, the probabilistic values should be increased. Increased probabilistic values can raise the ratings for a threat category or a security control test from low to medium, and medium to high.

11.4 Safeguard worksheets

The following are sample safeguard worksheets on password control (see Table 11.5) and contingency plan (Table 11.6). Both worksheets recommend the development of procedures to improve or implement the safeguards.

For each threat affected by the safeguard, savings are incurred by subtracting the revised expected loss from the original expected loss. Then, individual savings are added to give total savings for the safeguard in one stage of a development life cycle. However, there may be some cases where threats are listed in the worksheet but no savings are incurred as the software project moves from stage to another in a life cycle.

The cost of implementing the safeguard must be justified with a brief description. This description should include how the cost was determined and whether management objectives specify amortization of the costs. A ratio of the cost to total savings gives an ROI.

Table 11.5 Sample Safeguard Worksheet on Password Control

Safeguard Worksheet

Safeguard name		
Password control		
Annual cost	$200	
Description	Develop procedures for better password control management to counter the vulnerabilities of unauthorized leakage and unauthorized system access. Cost of this safeguard was estimated to be $200. Amortization of this cost was not considered. Management objectives specify that the implementation of this safeguard can be accomplished in one year or less	
Threats affected by this safeguard	Original Expected Loss	Revised Expected Loss
Unauthorized leakage	$13,000	$3,000
Unauthorized system access	$6,000	$1,000
Total savings	$15,000	
Return on investment	1:75	
Impacts on other safeguards	None	

Table 11.6 Sample Safeguard Worksheet on Contingency Plan

Safeguard Worksheet

Safeguard name		
Contingency plan		
Annual cost	$300	
Description	Develop procedures to prepare, write and test the XYZ Network System Contingency Plan. The procedures should include, at a minium, emergency response, and activities to allow the affected groups to return to normal operations in software development projects. The cost of this safeguard was estimated to be $900 and was amortized over three years, giving an annual cost of $200.	

Safeguard Worksheet

Threats affected by this safeguard	Original Expected Loss	Revised Expected Loss
System failure	$23,000	$3,000
Unauthorized hardware alteration	$6,000	$1,000
Total savings	$25,000	
Return on investment	1:83	
Impacts on other safeguards	None	

REFERENCES

[1] Karolak, Dale Water, *Software Engineering Risk Management*, Los Alamitos, CA: IEEE Computer Society Press, 1996.

[2] Ruthberg, Z. G., and B. T. Fisher, "Work Priority Scheme for EDP Audit and Computer Security Review," *Proc. of the 5th Asia Pacific Conference on Information Systems*, Hong Kong, Dec. 1989.

Chapter 12

Reiterative processes

R EITERATIVE PROCESSES in existing software engineering models are either limited in scope or virtually nonexistent. Conditions for continuing reiterative processes are undefined or not well defined.

To broaden the scope of reiterative processes, an approach is proposed to include the reiterative processes as an additional step in risk management processes for software engineering models. Reiterative processes are used to manage new risk factors and change risk prioritization in a software development life cycle and to improve continuously the quality of whole risk management processes.

Conditions for continuing reiterative processes must be defined and specific. They can change over a period of time or with a new set of management objectives. When conditions are met such as safeguards implementation, they result in improved quality of risk management processes and show better return on investments in economic value analyses.

If the impacts of changing conditions are complex, it can be tedious to perform by hand reiterative processes on prior steps in risk management processes. To improve the process of managing risks for large, complex software development projects, the entire risk management process should be automated.

Reiterative processes, automated or manual, can result in a substantial rework of software development processes. The issue of determining the limit on reiterative processes arises.

This chapter gives more information on existing and proposed approaches of reiterative processes and looks at advantages and disadvantages of implementing the automation. Then, the chapter discusses issues of reiteration limits. After this, it proceeds to sample data sheets impacted by reiterative processes, as well as feedback mechanisms.

12.1 Existing approaches

This section covers existing approaches to reiterative processes. Examples include Michael Purser's risk analysis process (see Chapter 5) and Boehm's incremental and spiral waterfall approaches (see Chapter 3).

12.1.1 Purser's risk analysis approach

Purser [1] gives a risk analysis procedure for securing data networking and briefly discusses the assessment of risks to some applications in banks and financial institutions, which are heavy users of security services. Purser suggests a reiterative approach that begins with the step of identification and selection of the safeguards. A risk analysis starts with the identification and valuation of the assets for a system. The identified assets are most likely to be exposed to a chance of loss or damage without the safeguards to protect the system. Each asset is assigned a reasonable replacement cost.

Next, risk analysis identifies management objectives on security for the system: client CAD/CAM workstations, a minicomputer, a local area network, or a wide area network. The objectives include the extent of protection needed for the system and the most cost-effective way of providing the needed protection.

Then, the analysis assesses the risks of threats to the assets and determines the measures of risk impacts to the assets. After this, the analysis identifies existing safeguards and assesses the vulnerabilities. The analysis proceeds to identify and recommend additional safeguards to protect the assets.

The implementation of the safeguards does not end the process. The process, now known as the risk management process, continuously receives the

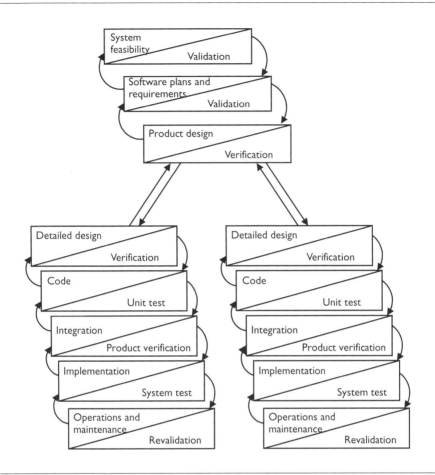

Figure 12.2 The incremental life cycle. (*After:* [3].)

Spiral life cycle

In addition to the series of "increments," Barry Boehm has discussed the possibility of developing and managing a software productivity system as a series of "spirals" (within the context of the culture of TRW Defense Systems Group). Unlike the incremental life cycle, the Boehm spiral includes objectives, alternatives, constraints, risk analysis, and prototyping in software development. It identifies and analyzes risks of alternatives for each spiral. Reiterative processes are implied in each spiral.

Figure 12.3 shows the "spirals" approach in the life cycle. The spiral is divided into four quadrants:

- *Quadrant I:*   Determine objectives, alternatives, and constraints;
- *Quadrant II:*   Evaluate alternatives, identify and resolve risks;
- *Quadrant III:*   Develop and verify next-level product;
- *Quadrant IV:*   Plan next phases.

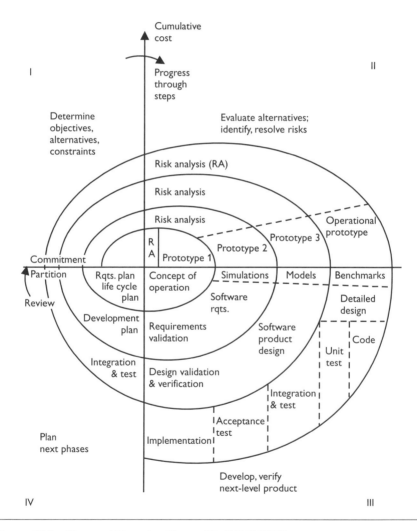

Figure 12.3   The spiral life cycle . (*Source:* [2]. ©1988 IEEE.)

The horizontal axis divides the spiral into quadrants I and II in the upper portion and quadrants III and IV in the lower portion of the model. It is obvious that the upper portion consists of the objective, alternative, and constraint determination components in quadrant I, the alternative evaluation and risk resolution component in quadrant II, the lower portion contains the product development and verification component in quadrant III, and the planning next phases component in quadrant IV. Planning next phase involves a review of the progress of prior steps and commitment of funds for the next phase.

In addition to quadrants, the spiral consists of four parts. Each is identified with a group function, as follows:

- *Spiral 1*: Concept spiral;
- *Spiral 2*: Simulations spiral;
- *Spiral 3*: Models spiral;
- *Spiral 4*: Benchmarks spiral.

The first spiral is the innermost spiral. Each spiral has its own set of determination, evaluation, development, and planning phases. For example, spiral 2 identifies the risks in alternatives of the requirements validation phase of the life cycle. Spiral 4 identifies the risks of the integration and test alternatives.

The concept spiral starts with the objectives, alternatives, and constraints in the first quadrant. It proceeds to risk analysis of the alternatives and prototype 1 in the second quadrant. The spiral then moves to the concept of operation in the third quadrant. It completes its round with the requirements and life cycle plans in the fourth quadrant.

Then, the spiral progresses to the next phase: the simulations spiral. This spiral requires another set of objectives, alternatives, and constraints for the requirements phase. The risks in the requirement alternatives are identified and resolved. The spiral moves to the third quadrant to develop and verify software requirements and requirements validation. It completes with a development plan to prepare for the models spiral.

In this spiral, objectives, alternatives, and constraints of the development phase are determined. This spiral identifies the risks of development alternatives. It proceeds to develop and verify software product design, design validation, design verification, and, then, to plan for the benchmarks spiral.

In this final spiral, the risks in integration alternatives are identified. It moves to the next quadrant to develop and verify detailed design, unit test and code, integration and test, acceptance test and, finally, implementation.

However, the reiterative process is not evident as the final component in the final spiral.

12.2 **Proposed approaches**

This section covers proposed approaches to reiterative processes, which is the sixth step of risk management processes. As shown in Figure 12.4, this step follows the steps of economic value analysis. The following topics are discussed:

- Life cycle;
- Feedback mechanisms;
- Forward and backward inputs;
- Reiterative versus repeatable processes.

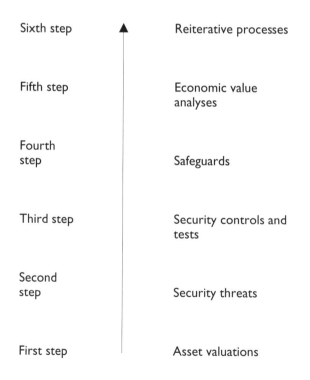

Figure 12.4   Reiterative processes is the sixth step in risk management processes.

12.2.1 Life cycle

Reiterative processes apply to any stage of the software development life cycle. The impacts and magnitude of the reiterative processes may differ from one stage to another. The differences depend on the complexity of the software development project in a life cycle stage and the impacts of evolving technology on vulnerabilities to the development project.

Figure 12.5 shows the impact of reiterative processes on other steps of risk management processes:

- Asset valuations;
- Security threats;
- Security controls and tests;
- Safeguards;
- Economic value analysis.

The whole risk management process is reiterative when the conditions change. The change may be permanent or temporary, external or internal, and involuntary or voluntary.

The risk management process is reiterative when:

- Serious risk incidents occur.
- Procedures on software configuration management undergo major changes.
- Management objectives mandate periodic reviews of risk management processes.
- Major or frequent modifications are required to correct or remove defects.
- A new risk analysis method must be implemented.
- A new algorithm shows a better way of calculating expected losses of the assets.

12.2.2 Feedback mechanisms

Reiterative processes include feedback mechanisms. Part of the output of a step in risk management processes and its external factors serve as inputs to that step (see Figure 12.6). They occur in response to changes in management objectives on the control of security policies, life cycle development projects, and quality improvement programs, as well as the implementation of technology evolution.

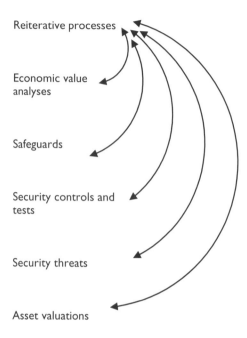

Figure 12.5 Impacts of reiterative processes on other steps in risk management processes.

The impacts of feedback must be economically significant in each step of risk management processes. Let's start with an example of changes in asset valuations which is the first step in risk management processes.

Major mainframe upgrades for a software development project require significant changes in asset valuations. The changes are economically significant. The feedback of asset changes result in the changes in asset valuation data sheets in the abbreviated risk analysis method.

Let's look at an economic impact example of security threats. An upgrade in data classification for the mainframe system requires significant changes in security threats. If the costs of the upgrade (e.g., from unclassified to secret) are major, the changes are economically significant. The feedback of the security threat changes result in changes in security threat data sheets in the abbreviated risk analysis method.

The same principles apply to safeguards data sheets. The addition of safeguards for large-scale migration of the mainframe legacy systems to a complex client/server environment requires significant changes in the safeguard component of data sheets as well as the savings justification sheets. If the costs of adding the safeguards are major, the changes are economically significant. The impacts

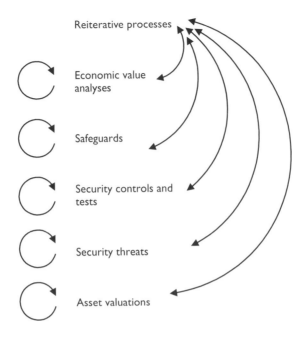

Figure 12.6 Reiterative processes include feedback mechanisms.

can change the mix of priorities of existing safeguards in the abbreviated risk analysis method.

The output of major changes in the asset valuations serves one of at least three inputs to the step of security threats in risk management processes. Part of the output from the step of security threats feeds back as a second input into that step. Changes in management objectives are a possible third input.

Likewise, part of the output from the step of security threats serves as an input to the step of security tests and controls. If major changes occur in security threat data sheets, part of the output will be returned to that step as an input. Other inputs are left to the reader's imagination. This includes part of the output from the step of asset valuations.

12.2.3 Forward and backward inputs

The output of one step, such as asset valuations, can be transformed into inputs to later steps. This does not mean that these inputs will occur at the same time. They could happen at different points of time. In addition, not all inputs will be applicable to certain software development life cycle projects. These inputs are called *forward* inputs.

In risk management processes, it is possible for a step to generate *backward* inputs. For example, if a new security threat is major, it may require a change or an upgrade in hardware and software configurations. Further, if the upgrade costs are economically significant, part of the output from the step of security threats becomes an input to the step of asset valuations. As shown in Figure 12.7, other parts of the output from the step of security threats could function as *forward* and *backward* inputs.

12.2.4   Reiterative versus repeatable processes

Reiterative processes are distinguished from repeatable processes in the Capability Maturity Model (CMM) (see Section 6.1.2 on organizational maturity in Chapter 6). Reiterative processes focus on continuous process improvement. It is at the upper end of risk management process.

On the other hand, repeatable processes look at the development of templates and procedures to standardize the process for a particular situation in the CMM. Repeatable process is the second maturity level of the five in the model.

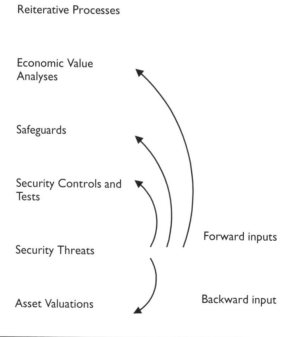

Figure 12.7   Part of the output from the step of security threats functions as forward and backward inputs.

12.3 **Automated risk management**

Risk management processes for software engineering models could serve as a framework for automating all steps of the processes. Automation can take place in any stage of the development life cycle. It is particularly important at the beginning of the life cycle. Errors and defects detected in early stages can be more easily corrected than those detected in later stages.

The automated software could be grouped into six modules. Each process module is identified with the name of a step in risk management processes:

- *Process 1*: Asset valuations;
- *Process 2*: Security threats;
- *Process 3*: Security tests and controls;
- *Process 4*: Safeguards;
- *Process 5*: Economic value analysis;
- *Process 6*: Reiterative processes.

For the first time, the process modules are sequential. When a process module is completed, it can move to the next higher process module. For example, process 1 can move up to process 2. The assets must be identified and valuated before security threats are identified.

Further, a process module cannot skip the next module for the next higher module. Process 1 cannot go directly to process 4 or process 5. Safeguards cannot be identified if threats are unknown. Likewise, an economic value analysis cannot be conducted if the information on security threats is unavailable.

After process 6 is reached, it is possible go from one process module to another in either direction, such as from process 6 to process 3, from process 2 to process 3, and so on. The time it takes to conduct reiterative processes should be reasonable to allow timely delivery of a software product and to remain within the budget.

All process modules would contain templates on data sheet formats and algorithms on probabilities. They should be flexible enough to accept user specifications for a particular development project and to incorporate changes in management objectives.

Despite the advantages noted above, there are drawbacks. They include the following:

- Unquantifiable risk elements (tangible and intangible);
- Human thought processes that may be not emulated;

- Automation that is not cost effective for small projects;
- Frequent changes in management objectives, requiring frequent automation updates.

12.4 Issues of reiteration limits

Gregory A. Hansen [4] suggests that "the risk of rework is often measured against the need to get to market quickly." The risk is that the products released to the market a little too soon are found to have bugs. Some bugs are "fixed" after the users have tested them. However, user testing is not always a reliable source of correcting the defects. Some products survive the bugs, some do not.

The point is that management objectives in software development organizations may limit the number of reiterative processes of "defect correction to meet schedules or control costs." As shown in Figure 12.8, schedules are impacted by organizational objectives, budgetary constraints, manpower availability, evolving technologies, and fast-changing market conditions.

To help the management to determine the limit on the rounds of reiterative processes, simulation of risk management processes in each stage of software development is recommended. Simulation can be accomplished with modeling of the risk management processes. Simulated processes should focus on measuring of the following scenarios:

Figure 12.8 Schedules are impacted by several factors.

- No prioritization of development processes;
- Prioritization of at least one process;
- Changing the mix of priorities;
- Changing workflow processes.

Workflow processes should include both tangible and intangible risk elements. Examples include project interdependencies, skill and training requirements, reorganization impacts, and changes in management objectives.

A drawback is that simulating the processes are more cost-effective for a large development organization than for a smaller one. However, simulating the processes should assist the management to determine the number of limits on reiterative processes for various types of software development projects.

12.5 **Sample data sheets**

This section gives sample data sheets impacted by reiterative processes and feedback mechanisms. They include data sheets on asset valuations and threats.

The impact column in asset valuation data sheets indicates the type of impact. A blank column indicates that the changes in asset valuations are a result of feedback mechanisms only for a particular asset. On the other hand, a nonblank impact category shows what process module results in changes for the asset.

For example, Table 12.1 shows the original hardware cost of $100,000 for the first stage. Table 12.2 shows additional costs of $100,000 to acquire new hardware. It is grouped into $50,000 for client/server upgrades to improve performance (feedback mechanisms) and $50,000 for hardware devices to counter new security threats (reiterative processes).

New security threats were discovered during security controls and tests (see Chapters 8 and 9). Examples include communication and power failure threats (see Tables 12.3 and 12.4). These threats denied service to 10,000–25,000 authorized network users. Several disgruntled employees flooded the system with files, records, and messages that dominated, stopped, or degraded the system. Power failure caused blackouts of the buildings as well as the servers, resulting in massive denial of service. In both instances, new assets were required to counter these threats.

The impacts of additional safeguards on the assets are then rated (see Chapter 10). The savings worksheets show savings incurred by subtracting the revised expected loss from the original expected loss. The expected costs of the losses are determined, for example, in a matrix format used to calculate the annual loss expectancy (see Chapter 11).

Changing conditions cause the reiterative processes to continue. Risk prioritization can change in each round of reiterative processes. Management objectives determine when the reiterative processes should cease at any point in risk management process.

The timing of releasing the product to a highly competitive market is crucial. If it is late, it may result in cost overruns. A prematurely released product may contain a high number of bugs.

In both instances, risk management processes for software engineering models were either poorly or not simulated. Management objectives were not clearly specified on the simulated use of risk management processes to meet schedules and control costs.

Table 12.1   An Example of a Data Sheet Showing Original Costs on Hardware Assets for Each Stage of a Development Life Cycle

Valuation Data Sheet: Hardware Assets	
System	Atlantic Warehouse Tracking Client/Server System
Location	Anywhere, USA
Total assets	
Development stage 1	$100,000*
Development stage 2	$110,000*
Development stage 3	$100,000*
Development stage 4	$100,000*
Development stage 5	$150,000*
Threat impacts	The hardware assets can be damaged or destroyed if adequate measures of safeguarding them are not taken, particularly for the servers
Replacement costs justifications	The costs are based on replacement costs for newer models. Technology evolves faster than the safeguards to counter the risks

* Detailed costs for each hardware component are attached to this data sheet. Quantity, device type, model number, serial number or other identifying number, as well as probability factors of cost changes are included.

Table 12.2 An Example of a Data Sheet Showing Revised Costs on Hardware Assets for the First Development Stage

Revised Valuation Data Sheet: Hardware Assets

System	Atlantic Warehouse Tracking Client/Server System		
Location	Anywhere, USA		
Total assets		*Additional cost*	*Impact*
Development stage 1	$200,000*	$50,000	
		$50,000	Security threat
Development stage 2	NA		
Development stage 3	NA		
Development Stage 4	NA		
Development Stage 5	NA		
Threat impacts	The hardware assets can be damaged or destroyed if adequate measures of safeguarding them against new security threats are not taken, particularly for the servers		
Replacement costs justifications	The costs are based on replacement costs for newer models. Technology evolves faster than the safeguards to counter the risks		

* Detailed costs for each hardware component are attached to this data sheet. Quantity, device type, model number, serial number or other identifying number, as well as probability factors of cost changes are included

Table 12.3 Sample Data Sheet on Intentional Threat Category on Communication Threats (Outsiders)

Additional Threat Data Sheet

Category	Intentional threat
Subcategory	Outsiders
Type	Communications threats
Scope	Masquerade and denial of service
Average frequency	100 times a year

Table 12.3 (continued)

Additional Threat Data Sheet

Historical damage	An outsider pretended to be an authorized user. About three or four authorized users flooded the system with files, records, or messages, thus dominating, stopping, or degrading the system, denying service to 10,000–25,000 users

Table 12.4 Sample Data Sheet on Natural Threat Category on Power Failure (Industrial Espionage)

Additional Threat Data Sheet

Category	Unintentional threat
Subcategory	Industrial espionage
Type	Power failure
Scope	Power source for file servers in main computer room
Average frequency	15 times a year
Historical damage	Power failure caused blackouts of the servers, denying service to 10,000–25,000 users

REFERENCES

[1] Purser, Michael, *Secure Data Networking*, Norwood, MA: Artech House, 1993.

[2] Boehm, Barry, "A Spiral Model of Software Development and Enhancement," *Proc. of an Int'l Workshop on the Software Process and Software Environments*, Coto de Caza, Trabuco Canyon, CA, 1985.

[3] Yourdan, Edward, *Decline & Fall of American Programmers*, Englewood Cliffs, NJ: PTR Prentice-Hall, 1993.

[4] Hansen, Gregory A., "Simulating Software Development Processes," *Computer*, Los Alamitos, CA, IEEE Computer Society, Vol. 29, No. 1, Jan. 1996, pp. 73–77.

About the Author

MARIAN MYERSON earned her M.S.E.E. in computer and information sciences. She is a computer/software engineer, a systems manager, a technical writer and consulting editor of computer manuals, technical reports, and textbooks. She has written numerous articles on data language and processing technologies for national trade publications.

Index

The Artech House Computer Science Library

For further information on these and other Artech House titles, contact:

Artech House
685 Canton Street
Norwood, MA 02062
617-769-9750
Fax: 617-769-6334
Telex: 951-659
email: artech@artech-house.com

Artech House
Portland House, Stag Place
London SW1E 5XA England
+44 (0) 171-973-8077
Fax: +44 (0)171-630-0166
Telex: 951-659
email: artech-uk@artech-house.com